THE HELEN KELLER STORY

"I think, therefore I am."
RENÉ DESCARTES

THE

HELEN KELLER

STORY

Catherine Owens Peare

THOMAS Y. CROWELL COMPANY

❈ *New York* ❈

I am indebted to Perkins School for the Blind in Watertown, Massachusetts, the American Foundation for the Blind, Inc., in New York City, and the Industrial Home for the Blind in Brooklyn, New York, for their hospitality and advice in preparing this book. I particularly wish to thank Nella Braddy (Mrs. Keith Henney), author of *Anne Sullivan Macy, the Story Behind Helen Keller*, and Evelyn Davidson Seide, personal secretary to Miss Keller, for reading the manuscript.

Excerpts from the following books are being reprinted by permission of Doubleday & Co., Inc.: *Story of My Life* by Helen Keller, copyright 1903 by Helen Keller. *Midstream* by Helen Keller, copyright 1929 by Helen Keller. *Out of the Dark* by Helen Keller, copyright 1913 by Doubleday & Co., Inc. *Teacher* by Helen Keller, copyright 1955 by Helen Keller. *Anne Sullivan Macy* by Nella Braddy, copyright 1933 by Nella Braddy Henney.

I am grateful to the following for permission to use material from the works indicated below: Appleton-Century-Crofts, Inc.: *Journey into Light* by Ishbel Ross, 1951. E. P. Dutton & Co., Inc.: *Phillips Brooks* by Alexander V. G. Allen, 1907. Methuen & Co., Ltd.: *Helen Keller in Scotland* by Helen Keller, 1933. Harper & Brothers: *Mark Twain's Autobiography*, 1906. Radcliffe College: four-line poem from 1904 Year Book. Arthur W. Blaxall: *Helen Keller Under the Southern Cross* by Arthur William Blaxall, 1952. (Council for the Blind, Pretoria). Helen Keller: *The Song of the Stone Wall*, 1910, and *The World I Live In*, 1908, both by Helen Keller. The Curtis Publishing Company: "My Future as I See It" by Helen Keller in the November 1903 issue of *Ladies' Home Journal*. The *New York Times*: brief passages from news items.

Foreword

HELEN KELLER was truly a remarkable person. Her personality radiated kindness, rare intelligence, and love for all mankind.

To know Helen Keller—as I did for more than a quarter of a century—was to love her and to draw inspiration from her. She was the living symbol of dedication to others. She planted the seed and tilled the soil which produced a better understanding and a greater appreciation of blind and deaf-blind persons, both here and abroad.

Helen Keller will always be a challenge to those who know the meaning of the word "handicapped." The handicapped were once considered individuals to be shunned because they were thought different, and Helen Keller, perhaps more than anyone else, helped to change this attitude. I think of Helen Keller as a great and good lady whose life was spent not only in overcoming her own lack of sight and hearing but in winning recognition for all handicapped persons.

In the pages that follow, Miss Peare has succeeded admirably in portraying the personality of Helen Keller, her generosity, her warm sense of humor, her profound sense of the beautiful. The book is refreshing in the simplicity of its style and the drama it unfolds. Here are all the essentials of Miss Keller's story: love, pathos, kindness, heartbreak, and, finally, triumph over great odds. It leaves the reader with the feeling that somehow all of us are, or ought to be, partners with Helen Keller—in helping others to help themselves.

Peter J. Salmon
ADMINISTRATIVE VICE PRESIDENT
THE INDUSTRIAL HOME FOR THE BLIND

Brooklyn, New York

Contents

1 ⁕ Pupil and Teacher

THE BABY WAS pretty and bright and quick. At six months she was almost talking. "Tea, tea, tea!" she said, or "wah-wah! wah-wah!" when she wanted a drink of water. By the time she was a year old she was trying to walk, a few steps and a tumble, a few steps and a tumble.

In the long, mild summers of the South, where shrubs and flowers grew luxuriantly, she learned quickly to love the out-of-doors. She reached out for dancing leaves, buried her nose in the roses, or cocked her head at the song of a bird.

"My daughter will be a lovely young lady some day," said her mother, holding the baby high. "She's a Boston Adams on my side, and her father is a Southern gentleman of distinction."

Captain Arthur Keller looked the part of a distinguished Southerner with his full mustache and goatee and straight posture. He had been an officer in the Confederate Army

1

during the Civil War, and he was distantly related to Robert E. Lee.

"I can scarcely believe he is twenty years older than I," Kate Adams Keller thought as she handed him his jouncing, lively daughter.

"My first little girl," he said, as the child tugged at his whiskers, "has a mind of her own."

Captain Keller already had two sons by a former marriage: James who was nineteen, almost as old as his stepmother; and Simpson who was in his early teens.

The little girl with a mind of her own had been born on June 27, 1880, in the town of Tuscumbia, Alabama, in a two-room house on the Keller farmlands where her parents were spending the first few years of their married life. The rest of the Keller family lived very near by in the main house, "Ivy Green."

"What will you call her?" had been the question of family and neighbors who crowded into the little annex to see the new baby.

"She is to be named after my mother, Helen Everett," said Mrs. Keller.

"I like the name of Mildred," said Captain Keller, but his remark was lost in the gay confusion.

When the day of the baby's christening arrived, Kate Keller looked proudly at her husband as he stood before the minister holding the tiny creature in a long white dress. But when the minister asked the baby's name, Captain Keller had a lapse of memory. He could remember only that she was to be named for her grandmother.

"She is to be called Helen Adams Keller," he told the minister, and Helen Adams Keller she became.

Kate Keller sighed and resigned herself to the error. Apparently her husband had a keen enough memory to be editor of their paper, the *North Alabamian,* but not keen enough to remember his own daughter's name.

Helen thrived and grew rapidly, passed her first summer, then her second, and her mother recited the old superstition, "When a baby passes its second summer, it is safe."

"Tea, tea, tea!" the baby chattered, as she became more and more aware of the world around her. "Wah-wah! Wahwah!"

It was during Helen's second winter, in February, that she was stricken and lay in her bed burning with fever.

"Acute congestion of the stomach and brain," was the diagnosis of the family doctor, which told them nothing at all. "I will not deceive you," he added. "I doubt very much that she will recover."

Kate Keller stayed with her baby day and night, soothed Helen's hot forehead with cool, wet cloths, whispered and hummed to her when she fretted. By some miracle the baby did recover, so far as anyone could see at the time, but the Kellers soon realized that the fever had destroyed Helen's sight and hearing.

Helen Keller became another kind of child. Since she could not hear, she could not learn to talk, and only emitted an occasional squeal or cry. Since she could not see, she became baffled by her environment, and would walk only when she could cling to her mother's long skirts. Because she was baffled, she became bad-tempered, contrary, hostile, unmanageable.

As she passed her second, third, and fourth birthdays, her disposition grew worse and worse. She wanted to communicate with the world around her and could not. She had devised a few signs of her own. She would nod for *yes* and shake her head for *no*. If she wanted bread and butter, she would act out the slicing of bread with a knife. If she wanted her mother, she stroked her cheek.

"She has intelligence," the heartbroken mother insisted. "I can see that she has intelligence."

But there were others who thought differently.

"You ought to have her put away, Kate," said one relative. "She's too odd to have around. The sight of her makes everyone unhappy."

She was certainly not a pleasant sight, even though she was a healthy, husky child, quite tall for her age. She was sullen and disheveled, often refusing to let anyone comb her hair or straighten her clothing.

All the while Kate and her husband inquired in every direction for doctors and specialists, the child's temper tantrums grew more violent, and her acts of mischief more dangerous.

Kate knew in her heart that she could expect to have the child taken away from her. What happened to a child that was "taken away"? Where would she be placed? Who would endure her willfulness like her own mother?

Captain and Mrs. Keller had moved out of the annex into the main house by the time Helen was five. Surely there was plenty of room for one handicapped child! And Mr. Keller had been appointed marshal of northern Alabama, which increased their income. Surely they could afford to give Helen some kind of care.

When Helen was six Mrs. Keller had a second child, Mildred.

Helen, surrounded by darkness and silence, was used to rushing to her mother's arms and her mother's lap whenever she felt insecure or lost or aggrieved. Suddenly there was another child in Mother's lap. Helen was accustomed to Mother's time whenever she wished, and now Mother was dividing her time, even pushing Helen away when she was attending to the new creature.

One day in a fit of resentment Helen darted at Mildred's cradle and tipped it over, sending Mildred tumbling out. Maybe the new child would break, the way her dolls sometimes broke when she dashed them to the floor.

Then, while the stamping and remorseless Helen felt hands pulling her away and guiding her out of the room, the distraught mother had to listen once more to the grim advice.

"You ought to put her away, Kate. She's mentally defective."

"No, no, no! She's intelligent. She learns easily. I can tell."

Something had to be done. The situation had to be faced and solved.

In the quiet of a late evening, when Mr. and Mrs. Keller were sitting in the living room and both children were asleep, an idea suddenly did occur to Mrs. Keller. She had been reading Charles Dickens's *American Notes*.

"Listen to this!" she said suddenly to her husband. "When Charles Dickens was in Boston he visited a place called the Perkins Institution for the Blind. He says, 'The children were at their daily tasks in different rooms, except a few who were already dismissed, and were at play. . . . Good order, cleanliness, and comfort pervaded every corner of the building. The various classes, who were gathered round their teachers, answered the questions put to them with readiness and intelligence, and in a spirit of cheerful contest for precedence which pleased me very much. . . . In a portion of the building set apart for that purpose are workshops for blind persons whose education is finished, and who have acquired a trade. . . . Several people were at work here, making brushes, mattresses, and so forth; and the cheerfulness, industry, and good order discernible in every other part of the building extended to this department also. On the ringing of a bell, the pupils all repaired, without any guide or leader, to a spacious music-hall, where they took their seats . . . and listened with manifest delight to a voluntary on the organ.' "

"My dear!" her husband interrupted her. "Have you forgotten that Helen is also deaf? Bells? Music halls? Organs? She could not be reached in that way."

"I know, I know!" replied Kate Keller. "But there's more. Dickens discovered something else. Listen to this."

Mrs. Keller read on: " 'The thought occurred to me as I sat down in another room, before a girl, blind, deaf, and dumb; destitute of smell, and nearly so of taste: before a fair young creature with every human faculty, and hope, and power of goodness and affection, enclosed within her delicate frame, and but one outward sense—the sense of touch. There she was, before me; built up, as it were, in a marble cell, impervious to any ray of light or particle of sound; with her poor white hand peeping through a chink in the wall, beckoning to some good man for help, that an immortal soul might be awakened. . . . Her face was radiant with intelligence and pleasure. Her hair, braided by her own hands, was bound about a head whose intellectual capacity and development were beautifully expressed in its graceful outline and its broad open brow; her dress, arranged by herself, was a pattern of neatness and simplicity. The work she had knitted lay beside her; her writing-book was on the desk she leaned upon. . . . She was seated in a little enclosure, made by school-desks and forms, writing her daily journal. . . . Her name is Laura Bridgman.' "

Arthur Keller had put down his own book and was looking off into space, thinking deeply as he listened.

"How did they communicate with her?" he asked.

"With a finger alphabet of some sort—entirely through her sense of touch, which is about all Laura Bridgman has. Helen is not as afflicted as Laura. Helen can taste and smell."

"I don't know," said Captain Keller. "Charles Dickens likes to dramatize things to the hilt. I think it would be wise to check up on the Perkins Institution in some other way."

A few days later a peddler came through town selling harnesses, and he knocked at the door of "Ivy Green." The minute Mrs. Keller heard his accent she asked, "Are you from New England?"

"Boston, ma'am."

"Have you ever heard of the Perkins Institution for the Blind?"

"No, ma'am, but I'll inquire about it when I return home," he promised.

Maybe he kept his promise; maybe he forgot. Anyway, the Kellers never heard from him again.

In a town as small as Tuscumbia everyone knew everyone else, and many of the neighbors worried about the deaf-blind child who was growing up half wild.

"I've heard of an eye specialist in Baltimore, a Dr. Chisholm," one of them dropped by to say. "He has cured many cases of blindness that were thought to be hopeless. Why don't you take your little girl to see him?"

Anxiously Kate Keller and the Captain took Helen on the long train trip to Baltimore, only to have Dr. Chisholm say,

"I can do nothing for her. She is permanently blind."

"But what becomes of people like Helen?" Mrs. Keller asked in desperation. "She won't always have us."

"While you are this far north," said Dr. Chisholm, "why don't you stop at the national capital on the way home and see Alexander Graham Bell? He knows a great deal about the teaching of deaf children, and he is a very sympathetic and understanding man."

With fading courage they went on to Washington, scarcely speaking a word to one another on the way, so sunken were they in black despair. A first child, a lovely child with silken, wavy hair, yet not a child, not really a human being.

Kate Keller thought Dr. Bell the kindliest man she had ever met. He was tall and attractive, with black hair and beard and large eyes. Not yet forty, he had ten years earlier demonstrated his telephone at the Philadelphia Centennial.

Dr. Bell put the Kellers at their ease at once and lifted the little girl to his knee while he talked with them.

"She's obviously a bright child, a very teachable child," said Dr. Bell as Helen explored his vest buttons with her fingers.

"Yes, Dr. Bell, but how? How?" begged Mrs. Keller, and she was almost in tears.

"Have you ever heard of the Perkins Institution in Boston?" he asked.

Kate and Arthur Keller looked at each other. Yes, they had!

"My wife read about it in Dickens's *American Notes,*" the Captain told Dr. Bell.

"Oh, then you know of the case of Laura Bridgman?" They nodded.

"The man who taught Laura Bridgman, Dr. Samuel Gridley Howe, is dead, but his successor, Mr. Michael Anagnos, is doing splendid work with handicapped children. I suggest that you write to him about Helen."

Both Kellers thanked him profusely. Their spirits had

risen steadily from the moment they had begun to talk with him.

"How did you happen to become interested in this sort of thing, Dr. Bell?" asked Mrs. Keller.

"My grandfather, my father, and I have all been interested in speech, in elocution, and in teaching articulation to deaf persons."

"It must be frightful to be deaf or blind," said Mrs. Keller.

"Oh, not necessarily," replied Dr. Bell in a very matter-of-fact tone. "My wife has been deaf since she was four, when she lost her hearing as a result of scarlet fever. We are very happy."

Kate Keller could have bitten off her own tongue for having said such a careless thing, but Dr. Bell didn't seem perturbed.

"The only thing we have to fear," he went on, "is ignorance, Mrs. Keller. In olden times the deaf-blind were legally classified as idiots, because no one understood them. We are beginning to overcome our ignorance of these matters. We are beginning to learn that what the handicapped need is education at the hands of well-trained and sympathetic teachers. Beethoven lost his hearing, you will remember, but he went right on composing music. Homer, the Greek poet, was blind. John Milton wrote his greatest poetry after he had lost his sight. And Thomas Edison, who has perfected the electric light bulb and is developing the electric power plant, is quite deaf. When he and his wife go to the theater, she taps out the dialogue on his knee in

Morse code. We really don't need all of our senses to live successfully."

Dr. Bell smiled at the little girl sitting on his knee, and he set his watch so that its alarm would ring and placed it in her hands. When she felt the vibration in her finger tips, she began to jounce and swing her feet happily.

"I can easily detect a great deal of intelligence in this little brown head," said Dr. Bell. "I am sure she can be educated. She is certainly bright enough to learn the finger alphabet."

The Kellers left his office filled with hope.

"Write the letter to Mr. Anagnos immediately," Mrs. Keller said as soon as they were home.

Captain Keller did just that, sending a detailed description of Helen, and a reply came from Perkins Institution very soon after. Before the summer ended, Mr. Anagnos had selected one of his own former students, twenty-year-old Anne Sullivan, to be Helen Keller's governess.

Anne Sullivan had come to Perkins as a blind child, he explained to the Kellers, and later her vision had been partially restored by surgery. She wanted to spend the winter weeks studying Dr. Howe's records on Laura Bridgman, before going to Alabama, and so they could expect her on the first of March.

"Just a few more months," thought Kate Keller. "Just a few more months, and there will be someone to take care of my little girl."

And while the robust and undisciplined Helen tyrannized the household with her pranks—locking doors and hiding

keys, yanking tablecloths filled with dishes to the floor—
Kate Keller fastened her hopes on Anne Sullivan and the
first of March.

"James will drive you to the station to meet her," said
the Captain when the day came.

Anxious and tense, Mrs. Keller sat on the front seat of
the carriage beside her stepson. He allowed the reins to lie
slack on the back of the motionless horse, and they both
stared along the railway tracks watching for that first puff
of soft-coal smoke in the distance.

"How will we know her?" Mrs. Keller wondered aloud.

"She will probably be the only passenger, Mother. It
will be all right. Don't worry."

"She is coming such a long way to help us!"

James noticed the train first.

"There it is," he said and climbed out of the carriage.

The train pulled in and ground to a stop before the
little wooden station house. A man in the baggage com-
partment tossed a sack of mail to the local agent, and the
train pulled out. No passenger disembarked.

Without a word James Keller climbed back into his
seat, jerked the reins, and turned the horse's head toward
home. Kate Keller fumbled for a handkerchief and began
to cry.

"What can you expect from a Yankee?" James snapped.
"I hope she never sets foot in Alabama."

"There's another train this afternoon, and we are going
to meet it!" declared Mrs. Keller firmly.

Anne Sullivan didn't appear on the first of March, nor
on the second.

"We are going to meet every train until she comes!" insisted Helen's mother.

On the third of March, 1887, Kate and James sat in the carriage at the railway station once more, waiting for a late afternoon train. This time a passenger did get off, a young girl dressed in burdensome woolen clothing, looking frightened and tired, her eyes red from weeping and the irritation of the soft-coal dust.

"Miss Sullivan?"

"Yes."

James helped her into the carriage, and placed her bag and trunk in the back.

"We were afraid you weren't coming," said Mrs. Keller.

"I am sorry," said Anne Sullivan. "I had the wrong kind of ticket somehow, and I had to change trains at Philadelphia and Baltimore. Then I had to wait over a whole day at Washington for a train coming to Tuscumbia."

"Oh, that is too bad."

"It's all right, now," said Miss Sullivan. "I'm only thinking of your little girl. I want to see my pupil as soon as possible."

The carriage drew into the yard at last and Captain Keller came forward to help them down. Miss Sullivan didn't seem to be listening to the introduction. She was looking at the open doorway of the house where a young mortal stood—blank-faced and hostile—nearly seven years old.

Miss Sullivan left the Kellers and hurried forward to gather the little "phantom" into her arms.

2 * Miracle at the Pump House

"PHANTOM"—HELEN KELLER'S own name for herself as a child—stood in the doorway sensing the excitement of a new arrival. She felt the vibration of a strange footstep on the porch, then another footstep, coming closer. Strangers were often enemies. She bent her head down and charged into the newcomer, and the newcomer fell back. Again the footsteps came toward her, and the stranger tried to put arms around her. Helen drove off Miss Sullivan's embrace with kicks and punches.

She discovered that the stranger had a bag, and she grabbed the bag and darted into the house. When her mother caught up with her and tried to take the bag away she fought, because she knew her mother would give in. Mother always gave in.

But Anne Sullivan encouraged her to keep the bag and carry it up the stairs. Soon a trunk was brought into the room, and Helen flung herself against it, exploring the lid with her fingers until she found the lock. Miss Sullivan

14

gave her the key and allowed her to unlock it and lift the lid. Helen plunged her hands down into the contents, feeling everything.

The newcomer lifted a doll out of the trunk and laid it in Helen's arms, and after that she did something very strange indeed. She held one of Helen's hands and in its palm formed curious figures with her own fingers. First she held her own thumb and middle finger together while her index finger stood upright. Then she formed a circle by joining her thumb and first finger, and finally she spread her thumb and index finger as far apart as they would go.

With a sudden wild leap Helen darted for the door, but the stranger caught hold of her and brought her back, forcing her into a chair. Helen fought and raged, but the stranger was strong. She did not give in like family and servants. Helen was startled to feel a piece of cake being placed in her hand, and she gobbled it down quickly before it could be taken away. The stranger did another trick with her fingers. On Helen's palm she formed an open circle with thumb and first finger, next closed her fist for a moment, following that by placing her thumb between her second and third fingers and curling her last two fingers under, and finally held all her finger tips together against her thumb.

That was enough! Helen tore loose and bolted out of the room and down the stairs, to Mother, to Father, to her stepbrother, to the cook, to anybody whom she could manage.

But at dinner the stranger sat next to her. Helen had her own way of eating, and no one had ever tried to stop her. She stumbled and groped her way from place to place, snatching and grabbing from other people's plates, sticking her fingers into anything at all. When she came to the visitor, her hand was slapped away. Helen reached out for the visitor's plate again. Another slap! She flung herself forward and was lifted bodily back. Now she was being forced into her own chair again, being made to sit there, and once more she was raging, fighting, kicking. She broke away and found all the other chairs empty. Her family had deserted her, left her alone with this enemy!

Again the enemy took hold of her, made her sit down, forced a spoon into her hand, made her eat from her own plate.

When the ordeal finally ended, she broke away and ran out of the dining room—to Mother, to Mother's arms. Mother's eyes were wet. Mother was crying. Mother was sorry.

Every day there were battles with the newcomer. There were battles when she had to take her bath, comb her hair, button her shoes. And always those finger tricks; even Mother and Father were doing them. Since the trick for cake usually brought her a piece of cake, Helen shrewdly began to learn others.

If battles with her new governess grew too unbearable, Helen could seek out Martha Washington, a child her own age, daughter of their Negro cook, and bully and boss her. Martha's pigtails were short because Helen had once clipped them off with a pair of scissors.

Or she could simply romp with her father's hunting dogs and forget there was such a thing in the house as a governess. She could help feed the turkey gobblers, or go hunting for the nests of the guinea hens in the tall grass. She loved to burrow her way in amongst the big flowering shrubs; completely surrounded by the prickly leaves of the mimosa she felt safe and protected.

There was real comfort in revenge. She knew about keys and locks, and she found a day when she could lock the awful intruder in her room and run away with the key. The big day of revenge eame when, in one of the enemy's unguarded moments, Helen raised her fists in the air and brought them down on Miss Sullivan's face. Two teeth snapped off.

An abrupt change occurred in her life right after that.

Miss Sullivan took her by the hand and they went for a carriage drive. When the carriage stopped, they alighted and entered a different house. Helen groped her way about the room, recognizing nothing, until her companion placed one of her own dolls in her arms. She clung to the familiar thing. But as soon as Helen realized that she was alone with the stranger in a strange place, that no amount of rubbing her cheek would bring her mother, she flung the doll away in a rage. She refused to eat, refused to wash, and gave the governess a long, violent tussle when it came time to go to bed.

The governess did not seem very tall, but she was strong and stubborn, and for the first time in her life Helen began to experience defeat. She grew tired, wanted to lie down and sleep, but still she struggled against the stranger's will. She would sleep on the floor, or in the chair! But each time she was dragged back to the bed. At last Helen felt herself giving in, and, exhausted by her own efforts, and huddled close to the farthest edge of the big double bed, she fell asleep.

When Helen awoke in the morning, she flung herself out of bed prepared to give further resistance, but somehow her face was washed with less effort than the night before, and after she had dressed and eaten her breakfast she felt her companion's determined but gentle hands guiding her fingers over some soft, coarse yarn, guiding them again along a thin bone shaft with a hooked end. In a very little while Helen had grasped the idea of crocheting, and as she became interested in making a chain she forgot to hate Anne Sullivan.

Each day in the new house after that brought new skills to be learned—cards to sew, beads to string.

After about two weeks, Helen had begun to accept her routine, her table manners, her tasks, her companion. The whole world seemed to grow gentler as her own raging disposition subsided.

She cocked her head suddenly one afternoon and sniffed the air, detecting a new odor in the room, something familiar—one of her father's dogs! Helen groped about until she found the silken, long-haired setter, Belle. Of all the dogs on the farm, Belle was Helen's favorite, and she quickly lifted one of Belle's paws and began to move the dog's toes in one of the finger tricks. Miss Sullivan patted Helen's head, and the approval made her feel almost happy.

Miss Sullivan soon took her by the hand and led her out the door, across a yard, to some front steps, and instantly Helen realized where she was. She was home! She had been in the little annex near home all this time. Mother and Father had not been far away. She raced up the steps and into the house and flung herself at one adult after another. She was home! Scrambling up the stairs to the second floor, she found her own room just the same, and when she felt Miss Sullivan standing behind her she turned impulsively and pointed a finger at her and then at her own palm. Who was she?

"T-e-a-c-h-e-r," Anne Sullivan spelled into her hand.

But the finger trick was too long to be learned at once.

Every day after that Teacher and Helen were constant companions indoors and out, and gradually Helen learned to see with her fingers. Teacher showed her how to explore plants and animals without damaging them—chickens, grasshoppers, rabbits, squirrels, frogs, wildflowers, butterflies, trees. Grasshoppers had smooth, clear wings; the wings of a butterfly were powdery. The bark of a tree had a curious odor, and through its huge trunk ran a gentle humming vibration.

Hand-in-hand they wandered for miles over the countryside, sometimes as far as the Tennessee River where the water rushed and churned over the mussel shoals.

For everything she felt or did there was a finger trick: wings, petals, river boats—walking, running, standing, drinking.

One morning when she was washing her face and hands,

Helen pointed to the water in the basin, and Teacher spelled into her hand: "w-a-t-e-r." At the breakfast table later Helen pointed to her mug of milk, and Teacher spelled: "m-i-l-k." But Helen became confused. "D-r-i-n-k" was milk, she insisted. Helen pointed to her milk again and Teacher spelled, "m-u-g." Was m-u-g d-r-i-n-k? In another second Helen's mind was a jumble of wiggling fingers. She was frustrated, bewildered, angry, a bird trapped in a cage and beating her wings against the bars.

Quickly Teacher placed an empty mug in her hand and led her out-of-doors to a pump that stood under a shed in the yard. Helen stood before the pump, mug in hand, as Teacher indicated, and felt the rush of cold water over her hands. Teacher took one of her hands and spelled, "w-a-t-e-r." While water rushed over one hand Helen felt the letters, w-a-t-e-r, in the other.

Suddenly Helen was transfixed, and she let her mug crash to the ground forgotten. A new, wonderful idea . . . back into her memory rushed that infant's word she had once spoken: "wah-wah." She grew excited, her pulse raced, as understanding lighted her mind. Wah-wah was w-a-t-e-r. It was a word! These finger tricks were words! There were words for everything. That was what Teacher was trying to tell her.

She felt Teacher rush to her and hug her, and Teacher was as excited as she, crying and laughing, because at last Helen understood the concept of words.

Joyfully they ran back into the house, and Helen was surrounded by an excited household. All the rest of the day she demanded words, words, words. What was this? What was that? Even the infant Mildred? What was that? "B-a-b-y." And once more Helen pointed a persistent finger at Miss Sullivan and demanded the word that would identify *her*.

"T-e-a-c-h-e-r," Anne Sullivan spelled. "T-e-a-c-h-e-r."

The last shred of hostility and hate vanished from Helen's soul as she glowed with her sudden happiness. She felt her fingers being lifted to Teacher's face to explore its expression. The corners of the mouth were drawn up and the cheeks were crinkled. Helen imitated the expression, and when she did her face was no longer blank, because Helen Keller was smiling.

When bedtime finally arrived, she put her hand willingly into Teacher's and mounted the stairs, and before climbing into bed she slipped her arms around Teacher's neck and kissed her—for the first time.

3 * Boston Bound

LEARNING BECAME A joy and a passion, and school was everywhere all day long. School was laughter and games and long excursions into the country with picnic luncheon under the trees. School was learning to climb trees, and learning the life cycles of the creatures who thrived in the long, warm summers of the Southland. The slim, slippery little fellow who lived in quiet, shallow water was a tadpole, who would some day grow into the large, cold frog with scrambling legs and a fat middle and smooth skin on his underside that pulsed and pulsed. The handful of hard specks were seeds. From each one a plant would sprout in the warm, wet earth, and the small plant would grow to a larger one until at last there would be buds, blossoms, fruit, and seeds again.

"C-i-r-c-u-s a-n-i-m-a-l-s," Miss Sullivan spelled into Helen's hand one day. "A circus is coming to town."

"What is a circus?" Helen wanted to know.

It was a most wonderful visitation of strange animals, and Teacher introduced her to them all. Helen explored the elephant's trunk and was lifted high on his back. She played with lion cubs, and shook the paw of a dancing bear. She even felt her way up the long, long neck of the giraffe until she found his head.

Helen wanted to learn everything—*everything*—and right away. Sometimes Teacher had to say, "Helen, I am tired."

Sometimes her mother or father said in alarm, "Helen, there is plenty of time. You cannot learn everything at once."

From the moment she opened her eyes in the morning she asked for words, words, words. She lived in a continuous state of excitement, and because she was so excited she often found it difficult to concentrate on her lesson. One day she made a mistake in arranging some beads in a pattern, and Miss Sullivan spelled into her hand, "T-h-i-n-k."

"What is *think*?" Helen wanted to know, and her teacher tapped Helen's forehead.

Helen grasped the idea at once, and that was her first abstract thought. It was followed quickly by another when Teacher spelled, "I love Helen."

"What is *love*?" asked the student, and that was not as easy as *think*.

Is it the smell of flowers? Is it the warmth of the sun? Is it when my heart beats? Why can't I touch love?

"You cannot touch the clouds, you know," said her

teacher, "but you feel the rain and know how glad the flowers and the thirsty earth are to have it after a hot day. You cannot touch love either; but you feel the sweetness that it pours into everything. Without love you would not be happy or want to play."

Helen began to understand.

One day Miss Sullivan laid in Helen's hand a piece of cardboard, and Helen could feel that the surface of it was uneven and filled with raised ridges. Teacher guided her fingers over the ridges and then spelled "d-o-l-l" into her hand. She did it several times. She gave Helen another piece of cardboard, and its ridges formed a different pattern. After Helen had studied the ridges, Miss Sullivan spelled into her hand the word "b-e-d." Next, teacher and student placed a doll on the bed.

In a very short time Helen was aglow with another discovery: words on paper, words spelled with raised letters. Soon she had a whole collection of cards, each with its word, and she and Teacher were playing an exciting game of making sentences by arranging the cards in a row. "Doll is on the bed."

But Helen was still Helen, still rebellious against her inability to express herself. She had discovered that other members of her family talked by moving their mouths. More than once she climbed into her father's lap and laid her hands on his lips to feel their movement. She tried to move her mouth the same way—with no results—and became so enraged by the futile effort that she flung herself on the floor, kicking and screaming.

And she was still a tyrant at times. One of the servants, named Viny, tried to remove a glass from her hands, fearing she would break it and injure herself, and the act brought on another tantrum. Teacher came rushing into the room, and Helen clung to her until her sobbing and trembling subsided.

"Viny bad," she spelled into Miss Sullivan's hand.

"You were very naughty," Miss Sullivan spelled back.

Helen was stubborn and would not give in, and as the day wore on she began to realize that she had made Teacher unhappy, so unhappy that Miss Sullivan did not eat any dinner. Gradually remorse overtook her, and Helen was able to spell the words, "I am sorry."

But as Helen's finger tips understood more and more, the world about her seemed safer, less baffling, and her temper tantrums were fewer and farther apart.

The more words she learned, the faster her schooling seemed to progress. One day Miss Sullivan laid before her a new kind of card, with parallel grooves but no letters. She laid a piece of plain paper over it and showed Helen how to feel the grooves through the paper. She placed a slim, round object in Helen's hand and spelled, "p-e-n-c-i-l." With Teacher holding her hand, Helen gradually learned to form the letters, words, and sentences she had been reading on cards. She ran to her mother, her father, her half-brothers for a hug, a kiss, a pat of praise and pride when she showed them what she had written, and by the middle of June she was ready to write her first letter, to a cousin named Anna:

helen write anna george will give helen apple simpson will shoot bird jack will give helen stick of candy doctor will give mildred medicine mother will make mildred new dress

There was only one difficulty with writing. Pencils left no ridges. She had to believe that the writing was there, and she had to remember what she had written.

Teacher was ready for this with her next step—another kind of card. Helen felt her finger tips being guided over the surface of the card. There were only raised dots. First, her fingers touched three dots in a vertical row, and then teacher laid her fingers on the raised letter *l*. With one dot added alongside the top dot of *l* it became the letter *p*.

"This is the printed language of the blind, Helen. This is braille."

Eagerly Helen learned letter after letter. The entire alphabet was made up of six dots arranged in different ways in a space, or cell, that was two dots wide and three dots high.

Braille printing was developed by a blind man named Louis Braille, Teacher told her. He had lost his sight in an accident when he was only three, and he had been educated by means of raised letters. When he was about twenty, he decided that raised letters were too clumsy, and he soon designed the system of dots.

Anne Sullivan had come to the Keller household on the third of March, and in July of that same summer Helen was ready to begin braille, so eager was she to learn; eager, that is, to learn to read and write. There were other lessons against which she rebelled.

Helen had discovered very young that her fingernails could feel no pain, that she could bite off the tips of them. Nail biting was something Miss Sullivan was determined to correct. Every so often Helen felt Miss Sullivan's hands take hold of hers and move them away from her mouth. It made her angry; she fought to keep her fingers in her mouth. But Teacher always won the struggle.

But it wasn't always nail biting even though it might seem so. Helen rushed to Teacher one day, sucking the tip of each finger, and Teacher moved her hands away from her mouth. No, no, no! Helen protested with great excitement. "Dog!" she spelled. "Baby."

"Did the dog hurt the baby?" asked Miss Sullivan.

No, no! Where were the words? Helen had discovered something wonderful. Teacher must come. She had groped her way into the well house and found one of the setters lying on her side. The silken, friendly dog licked Helen's hand as soon as she touched its mouth, but did not scramble to its feet. Running her hands along the dog's side, Helen quickly discovered why: a row of tiny creatures, their noses pushed into the big dog's side, sucking at her teats. Helen fairly flew out of the well house, across the yard, up the steps into the house to Teacher.

"Dog! Baby! Come!" And she sucked the tips of each of her own fingers in turn.

Together they hurried to the little shed and knelt beside the mother dog and her brand-new litter. Miss Sullivan took Helen's hand and spelled, "p-u-p-p-y." She taught Helen another word: "f-i-v-e." Five puppies, five fingers on each hand, *five;* and Helen had begun her numbers.

Counting became the new game. Every adult that Helen investigated had five fingers on each hand. Mother had one baby, Mildred. How many buttons on my dress? How many on my shoes? How many steps to go upstairs? Soon she was adding and subtracting beads on a string.

How many miles to Memphis? How many coins in my pocket? Helen's world grew bigger and bigger as she and Teacher traveled about. They went shopping in the big stores in Memphis, and Helen learned to use money. They visited cotton fields at different seasons and Teacher told Helen the story of cotton.

"Your dress is made of cotton. You wear cotton in Alabama because the sun is warm and cotton is cool. If you were in the North this late in the autumn you would have to wear woolens. Wool is made from the fur of the sheep."

How many miles from Tuscumbia to Boston?

"Boston and Massachusetts are much farther away than Memphis. I came from Massachusetts, but my mother and father came from farther away than that," Teacher told Helen. "They came from Limerick, Ireland."

Helen's vocabulary was increasing so rapidly that she understood almost everything Miss Sullivan told her.

"We lived on a farm in a village called Feeding Hills, Massachusetts," Miss Sullivan went on. "Where we lived the fields were covered with white daisies and yellow buttercups in the summer and with snow in the winter. Sometimes my father told me Irish fairy tales."

"Tell me an Irish fairy tale," she asked. And Anne Sullivan told her many.

Helen could not forget Boston.

"Does Laura Bridgman live in Boston?"

"Laura Bridgman is a grown lady now, teaching blind children at the Perkins Institution in Boston. Do you remember the doll I brought you when I first arrived? Laura Bridgman dressed it for you."

"Are there many blind children at Perkins?"

"Yes, there are quite a few."

"Can I write to them?"

"Yes, indeed; and one of these days you will meet them."

Then Teacher told her about Mr. Michael Anagnos, Director of the Perkins Institution, and about Alexander Graham Bell. Helen decided that she would write to both gentlemen, since they were her special friends.

Tuscumbia, November, 1887

dear mr. anagnos I will write you a letter. I and teacher did have pictures. teacher will send it to you. photographer does make pictures. carpenter does build new houses. gardener does dig and hoe ground and plant vegetables. my doll nancy is sleeping. . . .

Tuscumbia, November, 1887

Dear Mr. Bell.

I am glad to write you a letter. Father will send you picture. I and Father and Mother did go to see you in Washington. I did play with your watch. I do love you. . . . I can read stories in my book. I can write and spell and count. good girl. My sister can walk and run. . . .

Teacher had not only showed her how to play with her baby sister but she had brought her other playmates as well. Many of the neighborhood children were learning the finger alphabet, and when December appeared on the calendar, they ran to Helen and spelled into her hand, "C-h-r-i-s-t-m-a-s." This was really to be Helen's first Christmas. For the first time in her life she understood the secret plans, the hidden gifts; and there was to be a Christmas Eve party at the schoolhouse, *and she was invited.*

"T-r-e-e," the school children said to Helen, and Miss Sullivan explained that there was to be a big Christmas tree covered with beauty.

The other children took her by both hands and led her to their tree and let her explore all around it with her fingers. Helen knew trees as they grew wild, but this one was decorated with wonderful objects: round, smooth balls, fluffy cotton figures, strings of beads, and here and there a glow of warmth told her it was lighted with candles.

"They want you to give out the presents," Anne Sullivan told Helen, and Helen became an excited child among excited children, rushing happily about, bestowing treasures.

Back at home, Helen hung up her stocking before she went to bed.

"Santa Claus will come while you are asleep," Miss Sullivan promised.

Helen was the first awake next morning, and the first to come downstairs. As she felt her way about the room she discovered that the stocking she had hung was stuffed full and that packages were heaped under the tree and all over the room. Some of them, she could tell, were the ones she and Miss Sullivan had wrapped themselves.

"Now?" she begged as each adult came downstairs.

"After breakfast, Helen."

And after breakfast the happy bedlam of unwrapping presents began.

"Here is my present for you, Helen," said Miss Sullivan, and she guided Helen's hands over the bars of a cage and in through its tiny door to the occupant.

"It is a canary, Helen."

Helen sensed the flutter of wings near her hand, and tiny claws fastened themselves about her finger. The smallest and tamest bird she had ever known was perched on her hand. A live pet all her own! A creature to care for the way Miss Sullivan cared for her.

Children who trooped into the house later in the day asked, "What is his name?"

"Tim," Helen told them. "Little Tim."

Little Tim became a member of the Keller family very quickly, and just as quickly he was gone. When Teacher came upon Helen groping inside the empty cage for her pet, she put her arms around her and talked to her carefully. It had been the family cat, Teacher explained, who could not resist the sweet morsel. That was the way with nature. Every creature had its natural enemy, and cats were the natural enemies of birds.

"We must accept these things, Helen. They are a part of life."

Teacher seemed to understand everything.

"The things that puzzle you now will some day be clear," said Miss Sullivan. "Now let us read a story."

Miss Sullivan had begun early to read short, simple chil-dren's stories to Helen.

"Very soon we shall read whole books together," she promised.

Helen often found her teacher at a desk writing on paper with a pen. Could she learn to do that? Of course, if she wished, but there were other interesting ways to write—on a braille slate or on a typewriter.

"What do you write with your pen?"

"I am writing to Mr. Anagnos. I am telling him of your fine progress. He is very interested in you, and he is com-ing to Tuscumbia to see you."

"But I want to go to Boston."

"You will go to Boston. I promise you."

Early in the spring Helen stood once more in the door-way awaiting the arrival of a visitor, just as she had once stood awaiting Miss Sullivan. This time the strange step that vibrated on the porch did not belong to an enemy; it belonged to Mr. Anagnos.

A gentle hand touched her head and guided her indoors. She felt herself lifted into an ample lap, found a beard that was longer and fuller than her father's, and a round, warm face. Mr. Anagnos began to spell into her hand. He asked her if she remembered Alexander Graham Bell.

"He has a watch," said Helen. "He let me hold it. I wrote him a letter!"

"You wrote a very fine letter," Mr. Anagnos told her, "and you have written fine letters to me. I want you to keep on writing to me. That is the best way to show me your progress."

"I am coming to Boston," Helen announced.

"Yes," Mr. Anagnos agreed. "It is all arranged. In a few weeks you and your mother and Mildred and your teacher will all come to visit my school and my students, especially Laura Bridgman."

"Do you have sunshine in Boston?" asked Helen.

"Indeed we do," said Mr. Anagnos, laughing, "and it is not so warm there as it is here in Alabama."

"Boston is near the ocean," Miss Sullivan put in.

Helen began to bounce with joy. She had been reading stories about the sea.

"Will we visit the sea?"

"We will do better than that," her teacher promised. "We are going swimming in the sea, and you are going to learn about the sand and the tides."

4 ＊ Human Speech

HELEN HAD NOT quite reached her eighth birthday when she set out with her teacher, mother, and sister, bound for Boston. They were going to stop in Washington on the way to visit Dr. Alexander Graham Bell. This time they would find him at the office of the new Volta Bureau, an organization which he had founded as an information center on deafness.

"And you will go to the White House to visit President Grover Cleveland," said Mrs. Keller.

Dr. Bell seemed much more real to Helen than the President of the United States. And even he was almost forgotten as Teacher spelled into her hand descriptions of the landscape that flew by the train window during the long hours of the trip: cotton fields, orchards, houses, flocks, stretches of woodland.

"I like to travel," Helen observed, and begged for more word pictures.

When they reached Washington, Helen discovered that she really did remember Dr. Bell, especially the shape of his beard. This time they talked rapidly to each other with their fingers. She told him of the circus elephant she had seen with the long, ridiculous nose, and he told her about lions and tigers.

She was discouraged later when she discovered that President Cleveland didn't know the finger alphabet. The President held her hands and patted her head gently. He was quite big around, and the buttons down the front of his coat strained to escape from their buttonholes. His face was round, with no beard, just a thick mustache above his mouth.

Aboard a train once more, Helen asked eagerly, "Is Boston next?"

"We shall not reach Boston until tomorrow," her mother explained.

"Perkins Institution is really in South Boston," Miss Sullivan added. "It is a big, six-story frame house that used to be a fashionable summer hotel."

When at long last they reached South Boston and the Perkins Institution, Helen clung to Teacher's hand as she was guided up a flight of wooden steps, across a porch, and along a corridor.

"Helen," said Teacher, "here is a lady who was my house mother, Mrs. Sophia Hopkins."

Helen groped before her and discovered that Mrs. Hopkins knew the finger alphabet.

"I am glad you can visit us," said Mrs. Hopkins. "After

you leave here you will spend your vacation at my cottage in Brewster."

Holding an adult by each hand, Helen went on to visit Mr. Anagnos.

"Can I see Laura Bridgman?" she asked immediately, and Mr. Anagnos took her to Laura.

When Helen reached out and touched Laura, she thought she had never felt anyone so gentle. Laura was making lace, and when Helen tried to feel the lace Laura pushed her hands away from it and spelled, "I'm afraid your hands are not clean."

Impulsively Helen reached up to Laura's face, and the dainty Laura drew back. When Helen tried to sit on the floor, Laura lifted her to her feet and spelled, "You must not sit on the floor when you are wearing a clean dress."

At the end of the visit Helen rushed to kiss Laura goodby and stepped on her toe accidentally. Laura reprimanded her once more: "You must learn to be more gentle."

"Come," said Teacher, "the other students want to meet you too."

They were Helen's own age, as sturdy and full of energy as she, and they groped for her hands so that they could talk with her. Their fingers flashed; they welcomed her into their games. When Helen finally returned to Miss Sullivan, she was dancing up and down with happiness. "I like it here! I like it here!" she spelled into Teacher's palm.

After they had been at Perkins a few days and Helen had begun to feel completely at home there, Miss Sullivan asked, "Will you show Mr. Anagnos and some of his visitors how well you can read a poem?"

"I can read," said Helen confidently.

Teacher led her up a few steps.

"Helen, we are now on a platform facing an audience. It is graduation day at Perkins. Here is a poem written in braille. I want you to read it with your left hand and hold up your right hand and spell it to the audience with your fingers."

"How can they tell if they are blind?"

"The students are blind, but the visitors are not. I shall watch your fingers and say it to them."

A frown clouded Helen's face for a moment. Teacher was going to talk with her mouth. But she rallied and gave her performance, gave it so well, in fact, that she felt Mr. Anagnos, Mother, Mrs. Hopkins, and many strangers, crowd around her afterward, patting and approving.

That night she crept up to her teacher and felt her lips.

"Talk," she begged, and Teacher made her lips move.

"I want to do that," said Helen.

For an answer, Teacher only drew her close and kissed her, and Helen decided that that must mean she could never learn to talk with her mouth. But actually it had meant something quite different. Teacher had decided to take her to the Horace Mann School for the Deaf on Newbury Street in Boston.

"Sometimes deaf children are taught to speak," Teacher explained to her. "You may be able to learn a few words. But remember that no deaf-blind person has ever been taught to speak."

Helen was deeply excited by her visit with the deaf children and their teachers, and she tried to learn sounds by placing her hands on the lips and throat of the adults; but nothing really came of it except that she could make a couple of easy sounds like *mama* and *papa*.

The experience lived on in Helen's memory. She wanted to talk with her mouth. *Mama* and *papa* were not enough. The blind children at Perkins weren't dumb. The deaf children at Horace Mann weren't dumb.

"You must not hope for such a thing," Teacher cautioned her.

But Helen did. The thought was never completely out of her mind.

With Teacher, Mother, and Mildred she visited Bunker Hill and Plymouth Rock and learned the stories of the Revolution and the landing of the Pilgrims long before it —learned the stories from Teacher's fingers.

At last the four travelers settled down in Mrs. Hopkins's cottage in Brewster on Cape Cod for a few weeks of vacation.

"Now I shall swim far," declared Helen, who had been practicing swimming strokes lying on the floor at home.

"Very well, we shall go swimming right away. Come and put on your bathing suit."

As Helen walked with Teacher out onto the beach she felt the fine, soft sand under her bare feet. It was washed clean by the sea, by the rising and falling tides, Teacher explained. The sand grew damper as she reached the edge of the water, and soon water swirled around her ankles. She curled her toes into the sand and ventured in a little deeper. Oh, this was delicious.

"I want to swim now."

"First, learn to float."

She snatched her hand free and ventured farther out . . . out . . . as the water deepened around her and lapped at her gently. But suddenly her foot struck a rock and she pitched forward, floundering with hands and feet, engulfed, confused, all theories of swimming forgotten. She was terrified, helpless, drowning—until Teacher lifted her back to her feet, gasping and spitting, furious at the indignity.

"Who put salt into the water?" she demanded.

Helen learned quickly to get along with the sea and to understand it, and she spent happy hours searching for strangely shaped shells, trying to adopt a live horseshoe crab. The sea gave her a feeling of independence because she could find her way along its edge alone, and by the end of her vacation she was able to float with real confidence.

The sea was not her only joy at Brewster. Teacher had begun reading real books to her, and there were long, lovely hours for stories. One of the first full-length books they read together was *Little Lord Fauntleroy*, by Frances Hodgson Burnett. Little Lord Fauntleroy did kindly things for others; Teacher, Mother, Father, did kindly things for her. The idea was new to Helen.

"Can I do things for others?" she asked.

"Of course."

And Fauntleroy had gone to a foreign land with castles and a different countryside.

"I am going to England and visit Lord Fauntleroy some day."

Teacher told her that there were many foreign lands with curious buildings and strange customs.

"I shall go to all of them," Helen predicted.

They read *Heidi* that summer, and *Black Beauty*, and a great deal of poetry.

"Read some more!" Helen begged, and once Teacher said, "I must rest my eyes for a little while."

Then Helen noticed something that she hadn't noticed before. Teacher was wearing some sort of hard covering over her eyes.

"They are dark glasses," Miss Sullivan explained. "They protect my eyes from the strong light."

"Are your eyes sick too?"

"They once were like yours. When I was a child, I lost my eyesight, and that is why I went to Perkins to study with the blind children. When I was a young girl, a doctor operated on my eyes and gave me some vision. He operated again just before I went to Tuscumbia."

"Teacher will rest until we go home."

In September, after a short visit home, Helen Keller and her teacher returned to Perkins Institution, where Helen began her first days as a regular student, with Teacher sitting at her side to interpret into her hand.

She worked feverishly, passionately, at arithmetic, zoology, geography, reading, botany, history, gymnasium.

"You are a very determined little girl," said one of her instructors.

"I want to learn everything," she declared.

"You have plenty of time," she was told, but she couldn't understand that. Excitable, tense, imaginative, with a quick mind, she reached out her hands to examine everything shaped like a book and sought the raised dots with her finger tips.

One day on Mr. Anagnos's desk she found a large flat volume and made out the words *wie, schön, leuchtet,* in braille.

"What are these?" she wanted to know. "What do they spell?"

This was a book of songs written by a composer named Bach, Mr. Anagnos explained, and these words in the title were German. What was German? What was German? Mr. Anagnos and Miss Sullivan between them told her about other languages—Latin, Greek, French, German —and from then on Helen insisted on learning some words in these tongues. She loved languages, and it became apparent that she had a real flair for them. Soon her letters were sprinkled with foreign words. *"Mon cher Monsieur Anagnos,"* one of them began. To an aunt she wrote: *"J'ai une bonne petite soeur* is French, and it means I have a good little sister. . . . *Puer* is boy in Latin, and *mutter* is mother in German. I will teach Mildred many languages when I come home."

Helen wrote a great many letters, all in addition to her regular studies, and her correspondents made an ever-growing list of outstanding persons.

People all over the world were taking an interest in her,

and often gifts came to her in the mail from far away to help her learn of other lands and creatures: a large coiled seashell from one, a fossil plant from another.

The Reverend Phillips Brooks, rector of Trinity Church in Boston, became her personal friend very soon after her arrival at Perkins. He was known far and wide, and crowds came to his church every Sunday. Phillips Brooks wrote the well-loved hymn, "O Little Town of Bethlehem."

With Anne Sullivan as interpreter, the Boston minister and Helen held long conversations. She already knew many Bible stories.

"I always knew about God," Helen told Mr. Brooks. "I didn't know what He was called until I learned the word."

"The reason we love our friends is because God loves us," the great minister once told Helen.

"I shall bring you a typewriter when I return from vacation," said Teacher, who had been watching the increasing volume of fan mail and letter-writing.

Helen felt a sudden panic. Vacation? Return? Where was Teacher going?

"I must see a doctor about my eyes," Miss Sullivan explained, "and when you return to Tuscumbia for the summer I shall go away for a rest; in the fall we will be together again. Everyone must take a vacation, Helen."

"I shall write you letters all summer," Helen promised.

Tuscumbia seemed like a wholly different world when Helen returned to it after her winter at Perkins Institution.

Everyone seemed happier and kinder. Mildred was almost three, old enough to play, to be Helen's guide on walks through the woods.

Helen's vocabulary had increased so much that ideas fairly tumbled off the tips of her fingers. But they would tumble so much faster if she could talk with her mouth! The ambition to do so wouldn't let Helen alone. It popped into her mind when she was playing, or even when she was writing letters.

"Here is something to make you happy," said her father one day, and he laid a magazine in her hands.

She fluttered her fingers over it, but its pages were smooth and she couldn't read them.

"It is the September issue of *St. Nicholas*, a young people's magazine, and there is a story in it about you. Come. Let me read it to you."

He lifted her into his lap and spelled into her hand the story of her own life so far. The magazine went everywhere, he told her. Young people all over the country would become her friends after reading this. He described the photographs that went with the article.

"Here is a picture of you with one of our dogs."

Fan mail began to pour in after that, and Helen was busy answering it all the rest of her vacation. Even after she returned to Perkins in the late fall she had stacks of mail every day. Her new typewriter helped, but Teacher had to work along with her.

John Greenleaf Whittier, the Quaker poet, was one of her pen pals. To him she wrote:

Dear Poet:

I think you will be surprised to receive a letter from a little girl whom you do not know, but I thought you would be glad to hear that your beautiful poems make me very happy. Yesterday I read "In School Days" and "My Playmate," and I enjoyed them greatly. . . .

Whittier's reply was not long in coming, and in her next letter to her mother Helen reported joyfully, "I had a lovely letter from the poet Whittier. He loves me."

One day Helen pulled a letter out of the pile and sniffed at it. It had an odd, interesting odor.

"That odor is a special kind of tobacco, Helen," Miss Sullivan explained. "The writer is a gentleman in Hulton, Pennsylvania, Mr. William Wade. He saw your picture in *St. Nicholas*, and he thinks your dog is too small. He believes that blind children ought to have large dogs, and so he is sending you a mastiff puppy. That is the kind of dog his children have."

Soon another letter arrived telling Helen that the puppy had reached Tuscumbia safely, and Helen wrote at once to Mr. Wade.

My dear Mr. Wade:

. . . Thank you very much for the nice gift. I am very sorry that I was not at home to welcome her; but my mother and my baby sister will be very kind to her while her mistress is away. . . . I should like to call her Lioness, for your dog. May I? I hope she will be very faithful—and brave, too. . . .

As her fan mail subsided, Helen began to remember her disturbance about oral speech. The children at the Institution who were blind but not deaf talked freely with their mouths, and she was acutely aware of it.

One of her teachers, Mrs. Lamson, took hold of Helen's hand and drew her down beside her.

"You know," Mrs. Lamson began, "that I have just returned from a trip through Scandinavia."

Helen was interested in everyone's travels, but this time Mrs. Lamson wasn't talking about travel.

"I learned there," she went on, "of a deaf and blind girl in Norway, named Ragnhild Kaata, who is being taught successfully to talk with her mouth."

Helen became so excited that Mrs. Lamson could scarcely control her.

"It can be done! It can be done! How? Who will teach me? Will you?"

"It will take a long while," Mrs. Lamson cautioned. "You will find it very discouraging to practice and practice and fail and fail before you finally succeed."

"Who will teach me?" was all Helen wanted to know.

And she soon had her teacher—Miss Sarah Fuller, principal of the Horace Mann School for the Deaf in Boston.

"Try to be calm," said Miss Fuller, as the tense and eager Helen sat down with her for that first lesson in speech.

"Feel my mouth and throat carefully," said the speech teacher. "Now put your finger into my mouth and feel the position of my tongue. Try to hold your tongue in the same way."

After a few attempts Helen produced the sound of *i* in the word *it*, and Miss Fuller patted her on the arm.

"Now let us try another."

Helen's sensitive fingers studied Miss Fuller's tongue, teeth, lips, and soon she had produced the sound of *a* in *are*. She kept her fingers on Miss Fuller's lips and throat while her teacher started with the sound of *a* in *are* and gradually closed her mouth and said *arm*.

By the end of her first lesson Helen had learned six sounds: *m*, *p*, *a*, *s*, *t*, and *i*.

And everyone had thought this couldn't be done! She flung herself against Miss Sullivan as soon as the lesson was over, and they hugged each other happily.

There were ten lessons in all, over a period of about two months, and by the end of that time Helen spoke her first sentence, "It is warm."

She was still very far from talking, but she was on her way. *R*'s and *l*'s confused her and often became exchanged for one another. *Ch* sounds and *sh* sounds were troublesome.

After her ten lessons with Miss Fuller she continued to practice with Anne Sullivan, who herself had been taking lessons in speech teaching. Helen could not hear her own voice, nor anyone else's voice, and she could only utter a word and be corrected and utter it and be corrected, endlessly, until a pat on the arm assured her she had finally hit it right. Then she had to say it over and over and over to keep it right.

All this effort in addition to her regular school work! She was overtaxing her own strength and too young to have the wisdom to realize it. Those who were taking care of her could not have stopped her even if they had realized that she was overworking.

"You are losing color," said Miss Sullivan, "and that worries me. You are becoming nervous, too. I'll be glad when we can return to Tuscumbia for the summer."

"I shall be able to talk to my family when I return home this time," was all Helen could think about. "I shall be able to talk to my baby sister. And when I speak my dog's name she will come at the sound of my voice. Lioness! Here, girl!"

She was not dumb now! She was not dumb now!

5 * "The Frost King"

IN A WHIRLWIND return to Tuscumbia, Helen spoke full sentences to her mother, to her father, to Viny, to Mildred, and when her mother kissed her Mrs. Keller's cheeks were wet. To the half-grown mastiff that was waiting for her Helen said, "Here, Lioness! Here, girl!" And the huge dog bounded up in response to the voice, burying her muzzle in Helen's hands. Helen ran across the yard and called again, "Here, Lioness! Here, girl!" As quickly the dog loped up.

When Helen's family tried to talk to her with the manual alphabet, she pushed their hands aside, and insisted on reading their lips with her finger tips.

"I must practice," she told them.

But the long winter's work, the intense effort of learning to talk, took their toll of Helen's strength, and the humid-ity and heat of the southern summer did the rest. Helen was home only a few days when she felt her head begin to spin, and before she knew what was happening she sank to the floor in a faint.

There was to be no more studying or letter-writing for the rest of the summer, her family decreed; and so for a few weeks she did try to play and forget her work. She ran with Lioness and talked to her—"*mon beau chien*"—and renewed her acquaintance with all the farm animals. She and Teacher went on their favorite walks through the woods or down to the Tennessee River.

One day when they returned to the house from one of their walks, Captain Keller placed a letter in Helen's hand. One sniff and she knew where it had come from. It was from Mr. William Wade in Hulton, Pennsylvania. He wanted her to spend some of her vacation on his farm. He had a whole group of very tame and friendly donkeys, he told her, a pony that she could ride, and a gentle saddle horse for Teacher.

"And his children have a mastiff!" Helen remembered. "If I go, I can meet Mr. Wade and his children and the mastiff!"

"Of course, you may go," both her parents said.

The Kellers knew by then that Mr. Wade was a member of the iron manufacturing company of MacIntosh, Hemphill and Company, and that he owned extensive farmlands in Pennsylvania and a large plantation in Virginia.

When Helen and Miss Sullivan stepped from the train in Pittsburgh, Helen suddenly bolted toward a group of people on the platform and gave one of the men a hug.

"How did you know me?" asked Mr. Wade in surprise as she placed her fingers on his lips to listen.

"By your smell," she told him. "You smell just like your letters. Teacher says it is a special kind of tobacco."

"I am delighted to hear you speak," he told her.

"Can you understand me?"

"Sometimes; and what I don't understand Miss Sullivan interprets."

She felt his tremendous thick beard and mustache—and eyeglasses.

"Are your eyes sick?" Helen wanted to know.

"No. They are just not quite strong enough. These glasses improve my vision."

When they reached Hulton they found that Mr. and Mrs. Wade had three children, two sons and a daughter, and many persons working for them indoors and out. There was another guest stopping with the Wades, the Reverend J. G. Brown of Pittsburgh.

"I am planning to open a school for the blind in Pittsburgh," Mr. Brown told Helen. "Your friend, Mr. Wade, is helping me. He has been interested in the affairs of the blind for a long time, and now he is becoming interested in the problems of the deaf-blind."

Helen's heart melted inside her. A school for the blind! Affairs of the deaf-blind! Doing things for others, the new idea she had so recently discovered. The once violent little tyrant had become generous and thoughtful, although with her usual impetuousness she was going to the other extreme. When she and Teacher were out riding with the Wades and her mount proved too slow and sluggish, Mr. Wade put a stick into her hand. She wouldn't use it. She particularly watched for signs of fatigue in Teacher, and when Miss Sullivan finally said, "I am tired," Helen insisted that that was the end of the ride. She craved opportunities to do kindly things for others.

"You remind me of Little Lord Fauntleroy," Mr. Wade said to Helen. "I didn't believe in him until I met you."

"Oh, I believe in him," said Helen. "I am going to England to visit him some day. Ever since I read about him I have been trying to be like him."

But Teacher was watching Helen carefully, and when Helen became too goody-goody in her talk and actions, Teacher would say, "Don't be a little sermonizer."

"I want to be like Little Lord Fauntleroy."

"By all means be kind and generous, but don't preach or boast about it, and learn to laugh at yourself. Fauntleroy had no sense of humor."

After Helen had returned to Perkins Institution for the winter, she and Mr. Wade wrote frequent letters to one another.

"I am going to learn all I can about the deaf-blind," he told her, "and I shall need your help."

Helen was back at her letter-writing with great gusto. In December John Greenleaf Whittier must be congratulated on his birthday. "Eighty-three years seems very long to me. Does it seem long to you?" she asked him. The Quaker replied, "I do not wonder thee thinks eighty-three years a long time, but to me it seems but a very little while since

I was a boy no older than thee, playing on the old farm at Haverhill."

She must write to the Reverend Mr. Brooks and congratulate him on his promotion to the office of Bishop of Massachusetts, and later on in the year she wrote again telling him that her new brother had been born and named for him: Phillips Brooks Keller.

Mail arrived for her every day from friends and unknown admirers. Dr. Bell told her that he was founding a new organization, The American Association to Promote the Teaching of Speech to the Deaf, and it would hold its first meeting in the summer of 1891. There were many letters that winter from Mr. Anagnos, because he was traveling in Europe. "I showed the Queen of Greece your latest letter," he told her. "It made her cry."

She was going to Europe some day, and maybe she would meet the Queen of Greece. But in order to travel one must know a great deal. One must study and learn and read. Helen meant to learn everything that Perkins had to offer and then more.

Helen and her teacher visited the campus and buildings of the women's college in nearby Wellesley one day, and Helen startled Miss Sullivan by spelling into her hand, "Some day I shall go to college, but I shall go to Harvard!"

"First, complete your studies at Perkins," Teacher cautioned her.

She almost forgot her ambition to go to college when unexpected events during that winter at Perkins crowded it out of her mind. First a letter came from the Reverend Mr. Brown of Pittsburgh. He told her happily that his school for the blind had opened. But there was one thing that bothered him: the case of a six-year-old boy in Pittsburgh named Tommy Stringer. Tommy was deaf and blind as a result of having had spinal meningitis at four.

"I have been unable to obtain a teacher like yours for him," Mr. Brown said. "You see, he is a penniless orphan."

"I wish he lived near me so that I could teach him myself," Helen wrote back to Mr. Brown.

She began to worry about Tommy. Tommy must have a teacher. She told her many pen pals about him, especially Mr. Wade. It was all because he was penniless. Pennies? Would pennies do it? She talked to her classmates, and at last reported to Mr. Brown:

"Tommy will have a teacher some day, because we are raising the money to bring him to Perkins. My friends and I are saving our pennies, and I am giving up soda pop."

While she was working on Tommy's fund, another unhappy incident disturbed her.

"I have a letter from home, Helen," said Miss Sullivan. "It contains some sad news. Are you ready to hear it?"

Miss Sullivan always tried to tell Helen everything with absolute truthfulness.

"I am afraid something has happened to Lioness, Helen."

Helen grew tense as Miss Sullivan went on spelling into her hand. "You know that Lioness is a very large dog, and many people are afraid of her even though she is so gentle. Well, she was running free in the public park and one of the town policemen shot her."

"Is Lioness dead? Is she gone?"

"Yes, she is, Helen."

Helen buried her face in Anne Sullivan's neck and cried. Later, when she felt calmer, she comforted herself by writing to her friends about the accident. The first letter went to the man who had given her the dog, Mr. Wade: "I am sure they never could have done it, if they had only known what a dear good dog Lioness was!"

"I am sending you another dog," he replied at once.

He did something else, too. He sent Helen's letter to a sportsmen's magazine called *Forest and Stream*, and they published it in their section on dogs. Dog lovers everywhere read it and were enraged, and they began to send her offers of all sorts of dogs. A man in Quebec, Canada, began a subscription to buy her a new mastiff, and the editor of a London paper said he would make up any difference that was lacking.

Earnestly she began to answer them all, to tell them that Mr. Wade had already given her a dog, to thank them.

Suddenly a wonderful idea hit her. The world was full of generous people who wanted to help her. She didn't need the help, but someone else did—Tommy Stringer! She began to write letter after letter to all the people who had offered her donations of money or dogs—to the man in Canada, to the editor in London, to the many, many readers of *Forest and Stream*—to ask them if they would divert their help to Tommy.

"He is penniless. If I could collect enough money, he could come to Perkins and learn to be happy."

In a few weeks she had received three hundred dollars.

"Is this enough?" she asked Mr. Anagnos.

"No," he told her. Much more would be needed.

She appealed to Bishop Brooks, and he made a stirring speech at a public reception. Soon the total climbed to six hundred, and Helen's letters of appeals and thanks began to appear in the newspapers. By spring she had collected more than sixteen hundred dollars.

"Is that enough?" she asked Mr. Anagnos wistfully.

"My dear girl!" he declared happily. "That is enough to take care of Tommy for two years."

"I liked doing that," she said. "I liked helping a handicapped child. I am going to do it again sometime."

Eagerly she awaited news of Tommy. When he was first brought to Perkins, he was a "mere lump of clay that breathed," unable to do anything for himself. He had not even learned to walk, although he was nearly seven, because no one had known how to teach him. But at Perkins, with specially trained teachers, he quickly learned to walk, to dress and feed himself properly, and to talk with his fingers.

"What was his first word?" Helen wanted to know, remembering that *water* had turned the trick for her.

"*Bread,*" they told her. "He understood what bread was, and we soon made him understand that there was a word for it and for everything."

"You must teach him to speak!" she insisted, and they assured her that they would try very soon.

That spring she returned to Tuscumbia with a heart brimming with happiness. Tommy was taken care of, and she had a new dog.

More than her dog was waiting for her. Captain Keller led her up to a trim, gentle pony with a warm, silky coat.

"He is yours, Helen," said her father.

"What color is he? What color is he?"

"He is jet black, and there is a white star on his forehead."

"Black Beauty!"

And so a great part of her time that summer was spent trotting about on Black Beauty, with the second mastiff, almost as big as the pony, loping along on one side, while Teacher or another member of her family rode on the other side. The rest of her hours were spent at her other favorite pastimes: practicing speech, reading, and writing.

She was developing a rather good literary style of her own, and her stories and pieces were beginning to show a talent for writing. Some of them were published in the annual reports of the Perkins Institution. She wrote about everything and everyone—the climate, history, buildings, and geography of whatever country she was studying; real and imaginary playmates of her own age; fairy folk; experiences that she and Miss Sullivan had when they rode or walked through the Alabama woods.

In the late autumn when the leaves began to turn, Helen begged Teacher to describe their colors once more. Color was a constant challenge. She wanted to understand color. The sun was golden, warm; the leaves of the trees in summer were green, cool, pliable, and soft; in the autumn the leaves turned brittle, brilliant red and orange and brown. There were delicate differences in the odors of roses, and so she knew their colors must differ.

She understood sound; that was vibration. She could lay her hand on the piano when someone was playing and feel music. But color . . .

As her imagination mulled over the autumn leaves with their changing colors and tones, she began to have an idea for a story.

"It is a fairy story," she said, as she went to work on it, "about how the leaves change their color in the autumn."

Eagerly her family awaited the results.

At last she appeared at the dinner table, glowing with pride, finished story in hand—large sheets of heavy paper covered with the tiny dots of braille. Hands patted her with encouragement and admiration, and Miss Sullivan flicked a finger under her chin as a signal to begin reading.

Helen's speech was still very imperfect and almost unintelligible to strangers, but her family could understand her.

"King Frost lives in a beautiful palace far to the north, in the land of perpetual snow. The palace, which is magnificent beyond description, was built centuries ago, in the reign of King Glacier," Helen's story began. Like all kings, King Frost had treasures of gold and precious stones, and he wanted to make a right use of his riches. He decided to send his treasures to his jolly old neighbor, Santa Claus; he would know how to dispose of them. King Frost called together a troupe of fairies and instructed them to deliver the jars of precious stones to Santa Claus. The fairies started out on their journey, but they were merry little creatures who preferred play to work. They hid the jars among the trees and began to wander about hunting for nuts. While the care-less fairies were frolicking about, King Sun discovered the jars, and the stones of many colors began to melt and run away. Their crimson and gold colors dripped all over the leaves, and changed them to their brilliant autumn colors. At first King Frost was angry, but when he saw how beau-tiful the leaves were in their new colors he relented. "My idle fairies and my fiery enemy have taught me a new way of doing good." Ever since that time King Frost has taken great delight in painting the autumn leaves with glowing colors.

The Kellers were amazed.

"That is a very fine story," said Mrs. Keller. "What are you calling it?"

" 'Autumn Leaves,' " said Helen.

"It is an exceptional story, Helen," said Captain Keller. "Are you sure you didn't read it somewhere?"

"I did not read it," Helen protested. "It is my story for Mr. Anagnos's birthday."

Helen's smile vanished for a moment, but there were more pats of reassurance. It was all right. Helen was always surprising her family with her achievements. This story certainly showed that she had writing talent.

"I think 'The Frost King' would be a better title," said Captain Keller.

The idea appealed to Helen, and as soon as the title was changed, and a final copy made, the charming fairy tale was ready for Mr. Anagnos.

"Would you like me to take it to the post office for you?" asked Helen's father.

"Oh, no," said the author. "I shall mail it myself!"

The happiness that the story had created in Tuscumbia was repeated in South Boston as soon as Mr. Anagnos had read it. Mr. Anagnos was truly proud of her. He was going to publish the story in the monthly magazine of the Perkins Institution.

No sooner had the story appeared in print than a storm broke over Helen's head. Teacher gave her the bad news one morning as she was combing Helen's hair.

"Someone has written to Mr. Anagnos to say that your story is not original, Helen. The person says that there is a story called 'Frost Fairies' and that yours is the same."

Helen was seized with confusion. How could that be? "I wrote my own," she insisted.

"Do you remember ever reading 'Frost Fairies'? It was in a book of stories by Margaret T. Canby called *Birdie and His Fairy Friends.*"

Deeply troubled, Helen shook her head. No, she didn't remember any such book.

"I don't remember it either, Helen. I'm sure I never read it to you, but perhaps someone did."

Helen's spirit sank lower and lower as one after another said to her, "Try to remember. Try to remember when you first read the story."

"I never read it," she insisted. "I made up my own story."

Her life was suddenly filled with distrust, suspicion, doubt, embarrassment.

"Doesn't Mr. Anagnos believe me?" she asked. "Does he think I copied my story?"

She had to be told that Mr. Anagnos was deeply grieved and that he suspected her of dishonesty.

Helen cried bitterly over that.

"Helen, Helen," said Teacher. "I am going to get to the bottom of this, if it's the last thing I do."

And Teacher did. "There is no copy of Miss Canby's book in Tuscumbia, and none at Perkins," she told Helen. "But Mrs. Hopkins does have a copy. Do you remember that we stayed at her house in Brewster the first time I took you to Boston?"

"I still don't remember it," said Helen.

"Mrs. Hopkins must have read it to you and you forgot it," said Anne Sullivan. "I think I know what happened. The story was read to you when you had been with me only a year. You couldn't possibly have known so many words then, certainly not enough to understand the whole thing. But the story impressed itself on your subconscious mind, and when you recalled it you thought it was your own."

The storm raged around Helen's head and grew all out of proportion. Helen and her teacher had to return to Perkins for a "trial," and Helen had to appear before a group of the Perkins teachers and answer endless questions. The questions were accusing, suspicious, and repeated over and over in many ways. Helen felt as though she were suffocating; her ability to speak almost vanished; her fingers could scarcely recall the alphabet.

When at last the ordeal was ended, Teacher led her away and held Helen in her arms while she cried and cried.

"It's all right," Teacher said softly. "You were very brave, and I am proud of you."

"I shall never write anything again! Never, never!"

Soon Miss Canby wrote Helen a comforting letter, and when other writers heard about the ridiculous affair they wrote to Helen, too. Mark Twain fairly exploded with anger, as only he could. He had not yet met Helen Keller, but he certainly wished to be counted among her admirers. Who after all was completely original? he growled.

In spite of all the illustrious comfort, Helen felt badly shaken by the experience, and she was afraid to write anything at all.

"How can I tell what is my own?" she wanted to know.

She was going on twelve, almost at her most sensitive age.

Dr. Alexander Graham Bell was grieved by Helen's unhappiness, and he joined with Miss Sullivan in trying to persuade and encourage Helen to take up her writing once more. So did Dr. Bell's assistant at the Volta Bureau, Mr. John Hitz. Helen was as fond of Mr. Hitz as she was of Dr. Bell. Mr. Hitz was a sweet-mannered, elderly gentleman who had come to America from Switzerland years before, and he had been Swiss Consul General in Washington before he became Superintendent of the Volta Bureau.

Mr. Hitz talked with Helen about writing, and listened while she explained her fears.

"How can I tell? How can I be sure, Mr. Hitz?"

"You can write about facts that no one else knows," he told her.

"How can I be sure what people don't know?"

"People don't know about *you*."

"Could I write about myself?"

"Of course! If you write the story of your own life, you

can be sure that you are not taking thoughts from anyone else."

Miss Sullivan and Dr. Bell patted her arm.

"It is just possible," Mr. Hitz hinted, "that *The Youth's Companion* would want to publish such a story."

Soon she was at it, with help and encouragement coming to her from every side.

I was born twelve years ago, one bright June morning, in Tuscumbia, a pleasant little town in the northern part of Alabama. The beginning of my life was very simple, and very much like the beginning of every other little life; for I could see and hear when I first came to live in this beautiful world. . . . [All the details of her life were faithfully given—her illness, the arrival of Miss Sullivan, her canary, her growing love of books, Miss Fuller, Lioness, Tommy Stringer—all, that is, except the Frost King incident.] I will here end this little story of my childhood. I am spending the winter at my home in the lovely South, the land of sunshine and flowers, surrounded by all that makes life sweet and natural; loving parents, a precious baby brother, a tender little sister, and the dearest teacher in the world. My life is full of happiness. Every day brings me some new joy, some fresh token of love from distant friends, until in the "fullness of my glad heart, I cry": Love is everything! And God is Love.

6 * On Paper Wings

THE YOUTH'S COMPANION bought Helen Keller's story, just as Mr. Hitz, Dr. Bell, and others had predicted, and Helen's self-confidence began to return.

She could do anything with words on paper, she realized. That was her world. Through it she could share her life with others. In it she could visit with the peoples of other lands and even other times, the heroes of ancient Greece, the characters from Shakespeare, the tribes of faraway jungles.

"How easy it is to fly on paper wings!"

She was going to go everywhere on her paper wings. She would read and write and read and write. And she was going to try to persuade everyone she could to let other blind and deaf children learn to read and write so that they could travel on paper wings.

"You mustn't overwork, Helen," her mother cautioned, and so did others, because Helen refused to spare herself.

Her appetite was good and she slept soundly at night, but she was growing very rapidly. At twelve she was five feet two inches tall and weighed 122 pounds.

"Why not finish your studies before you begin to work for blind and deaf children," Miss Sullivan suggested.

Oh, no! She must do both. Dr. Bell wanted her to visit schools for the deaf, and she was going to do that. And he wanted her to go to the Chicago World's Fair, and she was going to do that.

"And I am going to college!"

"Very few women ever go to college."

"Women are being emancipated these days. Some day they will all go to college, and some day they will vote. I am going to work for women's rights, and I am going to earn my own living, too."

The Frost King incident had made an adult out of Helen Keller. She began to think of her life years in the future. She must acquire all the education she could. She must learn to speak distinctly. She must *do* things that were important and helpful.

In the summer of 1893 she and her teacher accompanied Dr. Bell to the Chicago Fair, and of course Helen attracted a great deal of interest. She insisted on visiting every exhibit, and when it was explained that she could see only with her fingers she was permitted to touch fragile and delicate works of art. She liked sculpture best, and that was natural. At the Egyptian exhibit she sat on the back of a camel.

She and Miss Sullivan returned to Hulton, Pennsylvania, to spend the rest of the summer with the Wades. Mr. Wade was as determined as Helen that she should have as much education as she wished, and he had engaged Dr. John D. Irons, a learned minister, to teach Helen Latin and to help her improve her arithmetic. Side by side, Helen and Teacher listened attentively to Dr. Irons as he explained Latin verbs and nouns and Teacher in turn repeated his words into Helen's hand. When lessons ended there were long rides through the fields and woods on Mr. Wade's horses and ponies, his dogs racing along beside them.

But as Helen studied with Dr. Irons and depended on the finger alphabet, she realized that her biggest stumbling block was not what appeared on paper, but what did not: oral speech. She was disturbed at her slow progress in learning to speak distinctly.

"You must remember, Helen," said Miss Sullivan, "that most children begin learning to talk when they are tiny, and you didn't start until you were ten."

"I'll talk plainly some day," Helen insisted. "You will show me how."

"I am not a speech teacher, Helen," said Miss Sullivan. "Your mother and father agree with me that you must have some help from a specialist."

But where was the money to come from? Captain Keller could no longer pay Miss Sullivan's small salary as governess, let alone that of a trained speech teacher. Helen knew that her companion was remaining with her for no pay at all, because she didn't want Helen's education stopped, and it gave Helen one more reason for wanting to earn her own living—to make it all up to Teacher.

Mr. John P. Spaulding, of Boston, a wealthy sugar manufacturer and philanthropist, like thousands of others had been watching the Helen Keller phenomenon. When he learned that Captain Keller could not afford the special training she needed, he tactfully arranged some income for Helen and her companion, and plans were quickly made to enter Helen in the Wright-Humason School for the Deaf in New York City.

"How soon will they be able to teach me to speak plainly?" demanded fourteen-year-old Helen. "I want to talk so that everyone will understand me."

"Don't expect too much," Anne Sullivan cautioned her again and again.

But Helen did. She couldn't help it. All the way to New York her imagination raced ahead of her and pictures danced in her mind: Helen talking, Helen conversing, Helen moving her lips the way others did and expressing ideas.

Helen and her companion both lived at the school, and during her class hours Helen received instruction in lip reading and in cultivating her voice. The drills proved slow and tedious and discouraging. Helen and Anne Sullivan stuck to it day in and day out, and Helen did progress— a little. Oh, she thought desperately, this was going to take a hundred years!

Helen studied at Wright-Humason for two years, from October, 1894. In addition to speech, she had regular lessons in French, German, arithmetic, and geography. Her German teacher learned the finger alphabet, and soon she and Helen were spelling words back and forth to each other haltingly in German. German became Helen's favorite foreign language.

With her to the school she had taken a few books from her rapidly growing braille library: *David Copperfield* in five volumes, a set of Tennyson's poems, a Latin grammar in four volumes. Braille books are large and clumsy because braille takes more space on the page than ordinary type.

Among her books was another volume, a gift from Mr. Hitz: selections from the writings of Emanuel Swedenborg.

"Just dip into this now and again," Mr. Hitz had said. "Don't try to read too much at one time."

Swedenborg had been born in Sweden more than two hundred years before. His great interest during the first half of his life had been science, especially nature and the universe, and it eventually led him into a study of religion and God. He devoted the second half of his life to interpreting the Bible and Christianity and wrote more than thirty books on his religious ideas. Those who studied his works and believed as he did eventually founded the New Church.

Bishop Brooks had once helped Helen to understand God, but Bishop Brooks had died. Then she became friends with the deeply religious John Hitz, and he guided her toward the views of Emanuel Swedenborg. Swedenborg was to be an adventure for Helen for the rest of her life.

During their two winter seasons in New York City Helen Keller and Anne Sullivan lived a tremendously rich social life when classes were over. They met many talented and interesting people. Mary Mapes Dodge, editor of *St. Nicholas* and author of *Hans Brinker*, became Helen's permanent friend. So did Kate Douglas Wiggin, another author of children's books. And there were such men as John D. Rockefeller. Since Helen liked to go to the theater, she was especially eager to meet actors and actresses: Ellen Terry, Henry Irving, Joseph Jefferson. How could she "listen" to a play, they always wanted to know.

"Teacher spells it into my hand," Helen told them.

"We are invited to the home of Mr. and Mrs. Laurence Hutton this Sunday afternoon," Miss Sullivan said one day.

When Teacher and pupil arrived at the Huttons', the drawing room was full of people, all eager to meet Helen. Helen felt her hostess's hand guiding her to her place, Miss Sullivan at her side, while the guests came forward one at a time to meet her. Helen kept her fingers on Miss Sullivan's lips, and as she heard each name she said something in greeting.

"This is Mr. William Dean Howells, the novelist, Helen," and the deaf-blind girl laid her hand in his.

"And this is Mark Twain." Helen felt her face grow warm as she took hold of the strong, impulsive hand of the breezy, outspoken writer who had given the world *Tom Sawyer, Life on the Mississippi,* and *The Prince and the Pauper.*

Later, when introductions were over, Helen sat with Mr. Howells and Mark Twain. Miss Sullivan asked into Helen's hand, "What is Mr. Clemens distinguished for?"

"For his humor," Helen replied.

"And for his wisdom," Mark Twain added with make-believe modesty.

"And for his wisdom," Helen echoed gayly.

Mark Twain held her hand to his lips as he told her a funny story, and she laughed happily.

Helen's speech at that early stage was so "crippled" and unintelligible that it was heartbreaking to hear, and her voice had a strange, throaty sound. But she left no doubt in anyone's mind that she *was* learning to talk with her mouth.

Helen spoke often of going to college, and Anne Sullivan was her staunch ally. Helen had made her choice of colleges, too. It was to be Radcliffe. When asked why, she replied, "Because they don't want me."

It was true. The authorities at Radcliffe had made it quite clear that they considered the idea of a deaf-blind student impossible.

She received offers and invitations from other colleges that were willing to make all kinds of allowances and special provisions. She said *no* to all of them. To her the word "impossible" meant "do it," and she insisted on preparing for the Radcliffe entrance examinations. Since Radcliffe was closely associated with Harvard, the young women had to pass the same examinations as the Harvard men.

During Helen's second year at Wright-Humason, Anne Sullivan looked about carefully for a good preparatory school, and she chose the Cambridge School for Young Ladies.

No sooner had they settled on their choice of school, than the first big obstacle was thrown in their path. Mr. John P. Spaulding, their patron, died, and they found themselves suddenly with no income. But not for long.

"Helen's education must go on," said Mrs. Laurence Hutton, and she and William Dean Howells and others formed a committee to raise a fund. Mr. Henry H. Rogers, the financier who was a vice-president of the Standard Oil Company and a friend of both Mr. Rockefeller and Mark Twain, donated the biggest part.

"I hope that some day I shall be able to earn my own way," Helen said to Anne, when she learned of Mr. Rogers's generosity. "I want to earn enough for both of us."

Now that Helen was older, she and her teacher were more like close friends than teacher and pupil. There was really a difference of only fourteen years in their ages, and the difference was becoming less and less noticeable.

"You will, Helen, as soon as you graduate from college. Just remember what a special service you are rendering by your public appearances. You are arousing public interest in the care of the deaf and the blind."

The more Helen thought of other handicapped people, the more ambitious she felt to learn accurate speech so that she could some day talk to audiences. Her ability to speak had improved at Wright-Humason, but it was still not like other people's. Only those who were accustomed to her could understand what she said.

At the end of her two years at Wright-Humason, though,

she decided to attempt to speak in public anyway, with Anne beside her to interpret. The occasion was the sixth annual meeting of Dr. Bell's American Association to Promote the Teaching of Speech to the Deaf, held in Philadelphia.

With her usual impatience Helen hurried along eagerly to the task, until she mounted the steps of the platform. Then stage fright seized her. Her mouth became so dry she could scarcely swallow. Her throat muscles locked. Where were the words to come from? She must speak—somehow—she must convince them that the deaf-blind can be taught to speak. It rested with her alone. She must speak . . .

Gradually she forced herself to stand straight and still and utter the first words. Thank heaven she had memorized her speech. She could never have mustered any ideas now.

If you knew all the joy I feel in being able to speak to you today, I think you would have some idea of the value of speech to the deaf, and you would understand why I want every little deaf child in all this great world to have an opportunity to learn to speak. . . . I can remember the time before I learned to speak, and how I used to struggle to express my thoughts by means of the manual alphabet—how my thoughts used to beat against my finger tips like little birds striving to gain their freedom, until one day Miss Fuller opened wide the prison door and let them escape. . . . Of course, it was not easy at first to fly. The speech-wings were weak and broken . . . nothing was left save the impulse to fly, but that was something. One can never consent to creep when one feels an impulse to soar. . . .

By the time she had reached the end of her talk she had recovered her poise and self-confidence. She felt a rush of warmth from her audience that she knew must be applause.

"Everyone said I spoke very well and intelligibly!" she wrote to John Hitz, and others explained to him how it had been done. She had paused after each sentence, and Miss Sullivan had repeated it to the audience.

There was no need to write to Dr. Bell. He had been in the audience to witness the miracle in person.

After the triumph in Philadelphia, Teacher and student went to Brewster on Cape Cod for a vacation, and they spent the latter part of the summer in the village of Wrentham visiting Mr. and Mrs. Joseph E. Chamberlin. Mr. Chamberlin wrote a literary column for a Boston newspaper, and all sorts of interesting artists came to visit at his big, old-fashioned house. Helen and Anne met such persons as the poets Louise Guiney, Bliss Carman, and Richard Hovey; and Mr. Chamberlin soon became "Uncle Ed" to Helen. It was Uncle Ed who introduced them to the poetry of Walt Whitman.

The summer was not entirely gay and happy. During the last week of August Helen was told that her father had died at home in Tuscumbia.

"And I wasn't there!"

"We are often called upon to give up the people we love, Helen," said Miss Sullivan. "Perhaps there is some comforting thought in the book Mr. Hitz gave you."

She was referring to Swedenborg. Anne Sullivan was not interested in Swedenborg, but she knew that Helen found a great deal of help in him.

Swedenborg believed in eternal life, and so he did not fear death. God, he said, was the "light of heaven" within each of us. It was the influence of the "light" within us that made us want to live lives of service or charity to others, and it was the "light" that gave us comfort and strength in time of grief.

When Helen left Wrentham for Cambridge she carefully took her volume of Swedenborg with her.

Early in October she and Anne were established at 37 Concord Avenue, Cambridge, not far from their school. The Cambridge School for Young Ladies was in charge of its founder, Mr. Arthur Gilman. Mr. Gilman and his wife had also helped to found Radcliffe College.

Knowing how close Helen and her sister Mildred were, Mr. Gilman generously offered to teach both girls if Mrs. Keller would let Mildred come north. To Helen's joy, Mrs. Keller did consent, and the two sisters were together all winter.

This was the first time that Helen had attempted to attend a school with seeing and hearing students, and there were no special provisions for her, except that Miss Sullivan attended all her classes with her and spelled the lessons into her hand. There were languages to be studied— German, Latin, English, French—and history, geometry, and astronomy.

Helen was determined to keep up with the unhandicapped children. Like so many others, when they met Helen Keller for the first time, Mr. Gilman was surprised to see how hard and intensely she worked. During the first year he tried to give her as much help as he could, often reading to her after class.

Helen's only worry was how hard Teacher was working. She knew that Anne was straining her eyes, reading too many books to Helen, because Helen could obtain only a few of her school books in raised type or braille.

Mr. Gilman's concern for Helen increased until a difference of opinion developed between him and Miss Sullivan. Since Miss Sullivan never kept anything from Helen, she told her about it.

"He is afraid I am letting you work too hard. He doesn't know you as well as I do."

The year passed peaceably enough, but the following autumn matters came to a head at the Cambridge school.

"I want to talk to you about your studies, Helen," Mr. Gilman said soon after school opened. "I have decided that you are carrying too many subjects. You must plan to take two years longer to prepare for college."

"I can do it all!"

"I think not. I've decided to drop geometry and astronomy from your schedule."

"Please talk to Teacher," Helen pleaded.

"I am in charge of this school, and not Miss Sullivan."

Alarmed by the sudden turn of affairs, Helen hurried to her sister. Teacher was visiting friends that day, and they didn't expect her back until the next day.

"I am going to take you girls to my home tonight," Mr. Gilman soon came and told them. "Mrs. Gilman will look after you."

The two girls clung to each other in sudden terror. What was going on? Where was Teacher? No, no, no! They would not go to Mr. Gilman's house.

Wisely, he did not force them, but let them return to their own quarters, where the maid, a motherly sort of woman, said, "Mr. Gilman doesn't want you to leave the house until this matter is settled."

What matter?

"Now, girls, Mr. Gilman is a very fine man. You must trust him. I really think he'd make a better guardian for you than Miss Sullivan."

So that was it!

"Come and eat your supper."

"No!"

"No!"

They refused to eat a bite all that evening. All they did was cry and beg for Miss Sullivan.

Not until the next day did Anne Sullivan come rushing into the house to gather both girls into her arms.

"Sh-h-h! It's all right. Be brave. I've sent telegrams to all our friends: to your mother, to Dr. Bell, to the Chamberlins. I won't let Mr. Gilman take you away from me."

By that time Mrs. Keller was aboard a train bound for Massachusetts, and Mr. Hitz was on his way up from Washington. The Chamberlins came and took the two girls to their home in Wrentham.

The whole affair was straightened out quickly as soon as Mrs. Keller and Mr. Hitz arrived on the scene.

"I would not dream of letting anyone separate you from

Teacher," Mrs. Keller promised her daughter. "It would be a cruel thing for both of you."

"We can arrange for a private tutor for you to finish your college preparatory work," said Mr. Hitz.

Soon Mr. Merton S. Keith, who lived in Cambridge, was engaged as Helen's tutor, Helen and Teacher remained with the Chamberlins in Wrentham, and Mrs. Keller took Mildred home to Tuscumbia.

Mr. Gilman had implied that it would be impossible for Helen to be ready to enter Radcliffe in the fall of 1900, and "impossible" was all Helen needed to hear. It was now Mr. Keith's turn to be amazed at her ability to work and concentrate.

Geometry and algebra were her most difficult subjects. She managed geometry by having pieces of wire fashioned into the shapes of circles, squares, and triangles. Trying to remember the letterings of the figures and all the steps to the solution was a severe test of her disposition. Sometimes she could feel those almost-forgotten childhood tantrums taking hold of her once more. There were times when she did pick up the wire figures and fling them across the room in despair.

She was able to use a braille writer for her algebra. A braille writer is a machine something like a typewriter, except that the figures appear on the stiff paper in the raised dots instead of in ink letters. Whenever she used the braille writer she could run her fingers over the paper and reread what she had written.

Since there were so many people who could not read

braille, she had to use a regular typewriter for much of her writing. She used the Hammond machine because its type was on a removable metal half-cylinder. She could have a cylinder of type for each language—English, Greek, German. The old Hammond was almost the same as the modern Vari-Typer machine.

At last, during several hours of every day from June 29 to July 3, 1900, Helen Keller sat at her typewriter in the office of Miss Agnes Irwin, Dean of Radcliffe, writing her entrance examinations.

The results were exciting and thrilling to more people than Helen Keller had any idea. She passed everything— German, Latin, English, French, history, geometry, algebra —and she took honors in English and German.

She sat perfectly still when she was told the good news, feeling a deep, deep joy. Paper wings! She had spread her paper wings and soared above the heads of many who had no handicaps at all.

7 * Radcliffe

FAY HOUSE, ONCE a private mansion, was the principal building of Radcliffe College when Helen Keller began her freshman year. Three stories high with rounded turrets on two sides, it stood facing a wide green lawn within a short walk of the Harvard campus. Near it were two small wooden buildings, and one of them housed the gymnasium. There were no dormitories then. Helen and Anne lived in a small furnished apartment in a frame house about a mile away, at 73 Dana Street.

With Anne Sullivan always at her side, Helen Keller walked the mile to her classes in Fay House each morning —dressed in the styles of the times. Helen enjoyed stylish clothes, and in 1900 the fashion lords decreed high laced shoes, a long, sweeping skirt, a shirtwaist with very stiff collars and cuffs, a hard sailor hat, and hair combed upward in a high pompadour.

Like almost every other lady of her day, Helen wore a watch pinned to the front of her shirtwaist. Hers was of a special design, though. It had an extra hand on the outside of the case that was connected with the minute hand inside and there were dots around the rim so that she could feel the time. The watch had been a gift from Mr. Hitz on her fourteenth birthday. He had purchased it long ago from a German diplomat, he told her. Its previous owner had had it designed so that he could tell time without appearing to look at his watch, since looking at his watch during an appointment would have been rude.

The classes that Helen attended in the various parlors of Fay House were taught by Harvard professors. There were classes in languages, literature, fine arts, botany, chemistry, economics, and government.

Helen and Radcliffe were agreed on one point: no special arrangements beyond having Anne with her to do her listening. She knew the professors were doubtful about the whole thing when she started her school year, and she felt those doubts rapidly disappearing as the term progressed.

She sensed the shyness of her classmates at first, and so she and Anne rather kept to themselves until the shyness wore off. It didn't take long. During her freshman year she was elected a vice-president of her class, and she held the post until her graduation.

Helen began to enjoy a real social life with normal young women. She donned the required full bloomers and middy and joined them in their games in the gymnasium.

She vied with them in swimming and went with them on picnics and hikes.

The high point of every week came at five o'clock on Wednesday afternoon, when Mrs. Louis Agassiz, President of Radcliffe, presided at tea in the first-floor parlor of Fay House. The wife of the great naturalist was seventy-eight and rather deaf, and the skin of her face felt withered and papery to Helen's sensitive fingers. Mrs. Agassiz had been one of the committee of seven who helped found Radcliffe, and she had been its active and vital president for more than twenty years.

Radcliffe tradition was dear to Mrs. Agassiz, and she liked to tell its history to the newly arrived freshmen or listen while upper classmen told it. Carefully Anne relayed the story to Helen. The college, known as the Harvard Annex then, had begun in 1879 with twenty-five "Harvard Girls." It grew so fast that it had to purchase Fay House, and just six years before Helen's arrival it had become Radcliffe College, named for Lady Mowlson, who had been Anne Radcliffe before her marriage. Back in the seventeenth century Lady Mowlson had given the first donation that Harvard had ever received from a woman.

Such conversations made Helen's pulse quicken. She was part of this progressive movement to allow women to have better educations. Not many women in America went to college, and she was one of those who did. In choosing Radcliffe she had chosen well. This was the place to begin her career: right here in the parlor of Fay House, taking tea with one of the most dignified and inspiring career women of the day.

During the summer between her freshman and sophomore years, Dr. Bell invited Helen and Teacher to spend their vacation at his place near Baddeck in Nova Scotia, Canada. She and Teacher and Dr. and Mrs. Bell spent happy hours walking along the shore or swimming, and there were many times when Dr. Bell and Helen sat talking alone. He was deeply concerned for her future and for her personal happiness. He told her that as a young man he had hoped for a career in music, and she told him that she hoped for a career in writing.

He asked her if she had ever thought of love.

"What made you think of that?" she asked.

"Oh, I often think of your future. To me you are a sweet, desirable young girl, and it is natural to think about love and happiness when we are young."

"Love," she told him, "is like a beautiful flower which I may not touch, but whose fragrance makes the garden a place of delight just the same."

He held her hand for a moment before spelling into it again, and then he said, "If a good man should desire to make you his wife, don't let anyone persuade you to forego that happiness because of your peculiar handicap."

She protested that marriage was not for her.

"You will change your mind some day, young woman, if the right man comes a-wooing."

The greatest part of Helen's time during her four years

at college was spent at her studies. At her apartment she had a growing library of books in braille and raised type. Mr. Wade was sending them to her as rapidly as he could have them prepared.

"Be sure to let me know what books you need," he had insisted.

Braille is not like ordinary type and cannot be printed as quickly. Braille printing is a slow and expensive process. To make it still slower Helen could not always find out far enough in advance what textbooks she was going to need for a particular course; then Anne Sullivan had to read to her from the regular text. This worried both young women because Anne was having more and more trouble with her sight. At times she had to hold a book almost against her nose to see the letters clearly.

"Teacher is sacrificing her sight for me," Helen thought, and begged her to have proper medical care.

Anne Sullivan did consent to an examination, and when the doctor learned that she actually read four or five hours every day, he fairly exploded.

"That is sheer madness, Miss Sullivan! You must rest your eyes completely if Miss Keller is to finish her course."

Her eyesight was failing, he went on. She would lose it altogether if she didn't take precautions.

Helen pleaded with Anne, but Anne Sullivan would not listen. Helen was doing something that had never before been accomplished in the history of the human race, Anne argued.

That was true! But why would Teacher not consent to having her eyes treated?

At last Anne did give way a little. She would undergo medical treatment provided it did not interrupt Helen's studies. For a while a young friend of theirs, Miss Lenore Kinney, became Anne's assistant and read to Helen for a few hours each day.

Helen's reading and courses were making it clearer each day that writing was to be an important part of whatever career she chose for herself: literature, languages, philosophy, English . . .

Her English teacher in her sophomore year was Professor Charles Townsend Copeland, and he encouraged her along the same lines that Dr. Bell, Mr. Hitz, and Anne had done —to write about herself. He soon detected that she was still afraid of being unoriginal, of unconsciously taking someone else's idea for her own.

"A writer must write about the things he knows, and you know yourself better than anything else. Don't forget what an interesting story you have to tell. There is no other like you in the world."

And so Helen delved into herself and gave Professor Copeland theme after theme.

One day, when she was sitting in Latin class, she was tapped on the arm and asked to step out into the corridor.

"Miss Keller, this is Mr. William Alexander of the *Ladies' Home Journal.*"

"We hope, Miss Keller, that you will consent to write the story of your life for our magazine."

"It is quite impossible," she told him. "I have a very heavy schedule of studies. There is no free time."

"You have already written a considerable part of it in your themes," he reminded her.

"How in the world did you find out I was writing themes?"

"It's my job to find out things," he laughed.

In a very short while Helen had signed a contract with the *Ladies' Home Journal* to write the story of her life in six installments. The magazine agreed to pay her three thousand dollars.

Three thousand dollars! Three thousand dollars! Oh, Anne, Anne! I can earn money! I can write and support both of us. Perhaps I can earn more than we need, and then we can plan to help others with it. Maybe we'll be able to travel, too.

The first installment of *The Story of My Life* arrived at the office of the magazine in Philadelphia, and the editors were very happy about it. This was certainly original material; no question about it; there had never been another of these.

Helen was excited and happy. She was finding it a little hard to concentrate on the task along with her regular studies, but it must be done. She managed for a while, but each installment went in a little closer to its deadline, and soon Helen began to panic. It wasn't possible! She couldn't! She should never have agreed. . . .

The *Ladies' Home Journal* became panicky, too.

Friends hurried to the rescue, the way they always did in Helen's life. They found at Harvard a young English instructor named John Albert Macy who gladly consented to assist Miss Keller with her task. He learned the finger alphabet quickly and worked diligently with Helen Keller to organize and edit the material that she wrote. They got on very well together, and the magazine editors relaxed as they saw their installments arriving in the mail on time.

John Macy did much more. He continued to work with Helen Keller on *The Story of My Life* so that it could be brought out in book form. Doubleday, Page & Company were to be her publishers. Eventually both brothers, Frank and Russell Doubleday, became her devoted friends.

When Mr. Wade learned that she wanted to read the manuscript through as one piece before sending it to Doubleday, Page, he arranged to have the whole thing copied in braille for her. Thus, she was able to make a few more revisions before turning it in.

The Story of My Life came out as a book in the spring of her junior year, and it was a best seller at once. It is still selling today. She found herself in a snowstorm of reviews and fan letters. Edward Everett Hale wrote to say that it was as great as *Kim* by Rudyard Kipling. Mark Twain's letter said, "You are a wonderful creature, the most wonderful in the world—you and your other half together—Miss Sullivan."

There were a few unkind jabs from those who refused to believe she had done it herself, or insisted that it was Miss Sullivan's achievement and not Helen's. She talked about sunshine, moonlight, color, flying birds! How could she know about these things? demanded her critics.

John Albert Macy, who by now knew better than anyone

that Helen Keller was a genius who had written her own material, took upon himself the task of replying to her critics:

> Helen Keller does use words which mean to other people something which she cannot know just as we know it. What these words mean to her, we cannot say without consulting her, and it is obviously difficult for her to tell us. There is no special vocabulary for the deaf-blind. If there were, we who see and hear could not be sure we understood it. The deaf-blind person must use as best he can the vocabulary made for him by a race with eyes and ears.

The unkind criticisms were not so many that Helen could not forget them in the light of all the wonderful comment she received. She knew what she meant when she spoke of color; she knew by association. "White is exalted and pure, green is exuberant, red suggests love or shame or strength." She had senses that the seeing and hearing forgot to use—the sense of smell, for instance. She could always tell where she was by an odor, even a faint scent, of hay, pines, flowers; indoors there were the odors of draperies, perfumes, lamplight, cooking. She had acutely seeing fingers that gave her images and shapes. Most important of all, she had "inward visions," visions called up by the poetry she read, by the thoughts she gleaned from her books, and from the writings of Swedenborg.

Swedenborg gave her her direction. "He brings fresh testimony to support our hope that the veil shall be drawn from unseeing eyes, that the dull ear shall be quickened, and dumb lips gladdened with speech." He gave her an "inward vision" of service to others. Gradually he was teaching her to be serene, gracious, patient, and forgiving. "Love," she wrote of Swedenborg's ideas, "is the all-important doctrine. This love means not a vague, aimless emotion, but desire of good united with wisdom and fulfilled in right action. For a life in the dark this love is the surest guidance." Swedenborgianism was really a way of life, a philosophy for every day in the week. In order to be happy she must live a useful life with no thought of reward. Let the cruel criticisms fall where they would. With such help she could go on calmly loving and forgiving and serving.

She must think of the future; she must plan carefully to use the talents that had been allotted to her. At the beginning of her senior year, she and Anne Sullivan began to consider the first important question about their future: where shall we live?

They had learned to love the village of Wrentham, and when they heard that an old farmhouse was for sale there they looked into the matter. The house had eleven rooms and a barn. It needed fixing, but there were eleven acres of land and plenty of big, old shade trees. Both Helen and Anne liked the open air and country places where they could take long walks and have all sorts of animal pets.

"A retreat where I may think and write," said Helen.

She would be twenty-four by the time she was graduated from college, and she had already passed beyond the jurisdiction of her family. Her patrons had become her "parents" —hers and Anne's.

Mr. Spaulding had left them some shares of sugar stock; they sold the stock and purchased the house with the proceeds. They owned it together, and they made out their wills in favor of each other.

There were really three of them to be considered, because Helen's classmates had made her a gift of a Boston terrier—Phiz.

Helen's senior year moved swiftly, and as final examinations and graduation approached, she and Anne could scarcely believe that four years had passed. Their days had been so full, and they had worked under so much pressure to accomplish everything in the time allowed that the weeks and months had flown.

There were sixty-five young women in the class of 1904. In their yearbook, where an appropriate verse appeared about each name, they said of Helen Keller:

> Beside her task our efforts pale,
> She never knew the word for fail;
> Beside her triumphs ours are naught,
> For hers were far more dearly bought.

Helen Keller had not merely completed her college work in the prescribed four years. She was graduated with honors—*cum laude*.

8 ＊ I Shall Devote My Life

HELEN HAD OMITTED an important bit of information from *The Story of My Life*: her choice of career. The *Ladies' Home Journal* soon asked her for another article to fill in the gap, and the result was *"My Future as I See It."*

She must earn a living, she explained in her article, and her life must have a theme. "I could teach and perhaps write," she said. "I could take up settlement work. I could help care for the sick." She could certainly train to be a masseuse. Oh, there were many ways in which she could earn her living. As for the theme of her life, there was no doubt about that: the deaf and blind people of the world needed her. The public must be educated to understand them; its interest must be aroused in their welfare. The world was full of blind people whose sight could have been saved, and countless blind were living idle, dependent lives when they could be gainfully employed. Her recent trip to the World's Fair in Chicago had showed how much good she could do by personal appearances alone to dispel ignorance and despair. There were all the problems of the deaf as well, and no one knew how many deaf-blind there were. Sensibly realizing that she could not do it all, she made the necessary choice. "I shall devote my life to those who suffer from loss of sight."

"I am still a college girl," wrote the young woman bursting with ideals and ambitions, "and I can look forward to a golden age when all my plans shall have been realized. I can dream of that happy country of the future where no man will live at his ease while another suffers; then, indeed, shall the blind see and the deaf hear."

But before any careers or dream worlds could be launched, Helen and Anne had to retire to their new home in Wrentham to rest. They were both exhausted, mentally and physically, from their four years of effort.

During the months they had owned the run-down old place they had done a great deal to make it comfortable, and eagerly Helen brushed away Anne's guiding hands as she stepped into the front room. Her home, her own home, she thought fervently, as she felt her cautious way toward one room in particular. This was her workroom, created by knocking out partitions between two pantries.

"Here I shall write and write," Helen declared, running her finger tips over her typewriter.

She turned toward the stairs to the second floor, her finger tips gliding along the banister as she went up to her bedroom.

"There is a surprise waiting for you," said Anne, steering Helen toward a window.

The window had been made into a door that opened onto a wide and ample porch. Helen walked out onto it and explored its dimensions, feeling along the waist-high railing that surrounded it. Here she could exercise when the weather was inclement.

"And when the weather is fair," said Anne, leading Helen out of doors, and laying her hand on a wire, "you may stroll on the grounds."

Walking-wires had been strung in many directions over the premises.

"I can go out alone!" Helen said happily. "Oh, smell the wisteria, the evergreens, and the apple blossoms."

Phiz jumped around wildly. Here at last, he seemed to say, is space enough.

In a few weeks the two young women began to feel rested—then restless to be at work—then excited and ambitious.

"I have so many thoughts to put down on paper," said Helen.

Her college education had developed her ability to express herself, and it had helped her to know her own philosophy of life. She wanted to share all of this with the world. Her typewriter began to click through many hours of the day.

After she had written an article she turned it over to Anne Sullivan, who read it back to her so that she could make corrections. John Macy worked with Helen, too, from time to time.

She wrote about the subjects that she understood best: how she "saw" with her hands and how her imagination helped her hands to see; how the hands of others felt to her and how she judged character by a handclasp. She could remember that Bishop Brooks had had hands that were "brimful of tenderness and a strong man's joy." And Mark Twain's hand was "full of whimsies and the drollest humors." Some people's hands were weak, some strong, some fidgety, some brave, some timid.

She wrote of her own highly developed sense of smell, that sense that other people neglected. Hers was no keener than anyone else's, but hers had been trained through constant usage. "The sense of smell has told me of a coming storm hours before there was any sign of it visible." Strong, young men smelt to her like "fire, storm, and salt sea."

Century Magazine bought many of her articles, and so did such other magazines as *McClure's, Charities and Commons, Putnam's, Outlook, World's Work, Current Literature,* and, of course, *Ladies' Home Journal.*

Most important, she wrote articles on the problem of blindness: "How to Be Blind" for *Outlook;* "How the Blind May Be Helped" for *Putnam's;* "Unnecessary Blindness" and "Correct Training of a Blind Child" for *Ladies' Home Journal.*

She lived at Wrentham for over twelve years, and during that period she wrote a great volume of copy and watched its gradual effect as magazines began to give more and more space to articles on blindness by authorities in the field: articles discussing blindness in general, asylums for the blind, education of the blind, and employment of the blind.

She and Anne Sullivan had been at Wrentham only a few months when they realized that money would always be scarce, no matter how hard Helen worked at her typewriter. They could have a handyman for the out-of-doors work and only one servant indoors. Helen learned to do every housekeeping task possible to her—dusting, washing dishes, making beds, preparing breakfast.

One wonderful part about having a house, in spite of the work it involved, was having space for guests. Mrs. Keller and Mildred could come up from Alabama. John Hitz, well past seventy, came every summer. In spite of his advanced years, he had learned to read and write braille so that he could transcribe anything he thought Helen Keller would enjoy reading.

John Macy came oftener than anyone, to help Helen with her manuscripts and to read aloud to Anne Sullivan. Gradually, Helen became aware of a tension in the air whenever John Macy called, and aware that Anne felt depressed after he left. She said nothing about it, because she felt unsure, confused, troubled. Her deafness and blindness gave her the isolation and peace in which to think deeply and clearly, and at long last she arrived at the answer: John Macy and Anne Sullivan were in love.

With eager excitement she drew the story out of Anne a bit at a time, and what Anne did not tell her she was able to guess. Anne was refusing to marry John Macy, and John Macy was refusing to accept *no* for an answer.

Why, why? Helen wanted to know. Did she not love John?

Yes, she did. But Anne's life was dedicated to Helen. She could never leave Helen, never stop being her closest companion. Their lives were too interwoven to be separated now.

"Oh, Teacher," Helen exclaimed, "if you love John and let him go, I shall feel like a hideous accident!"

"He is much younger than I," Anne said a little lamely.

What of that? Anne was thirty-nine and he was twenty-eight. It wasn't as though she were nineteen and he were eight. They were both mature.

Helen talked with John, too; she wanted them both to understand how much she wanted them to be happy, how deeply she wanted not to feel that she had spoiled happiness for them. John was convinced; he felt impatient about Anne's indecision. He was not going to take Anne away from Helen, he said; he had no wish to.

Anne Sullivan changed her mind many times, but at last the date of the wedding was set for May 2, 1905. The ceremony was to take place in the Wrentham house, and Helen was to be maid of honor.

The party that gathered that happy afternoon was a small one, but it filled the parlor of the farmhouse. John Hitz came; so did the groom's parents and Mother Keller from Alabama. The Reverend Edward Everett Hale performed the ceremony. The happy couple left for New Orleans on their honeymoon as soon as they could get away, and Helen returned with her mother to Tuscumbia.

In a few weeks Helen Keller and Mr. and Mrs. Macy were back in Wrentham, where the three of them planned to live. John Macy was employed as an associate editor of *The Youth's Companion,* and his salary plus what Helen could earn with her writing, they hoped, would give them enough of an income to live on.

And it did—for a while.

The days that followed were happy and successful and filled with fruitful activity. Helen's articles continued to appear in magazines, and she made many public appearances. The Governor of Massachusetts appointed her a member of the state's Commission for the Blind, and she diligently attended its meetings.

The only sad incident during those first years at Wrentham was the death of Phiz, and Helen declared that she would never have another dog. Losing them was too difficult. Dogs simply didn't live long enough.

John and Anne exchanged a knowing glance. How long, the glance said, would it be before they would have to housebreak another dog? Not long at all. The next pet was a French bull terrier called Kaiser. After Kaiser there came Thora, a grand looking Great Dane, who arrived in time to have a litter of eleven puppies, all of whom had to be given the best possible bringing up and then placed in good homes. Out of the eleven puppies Helen kept one—Sieglinde.

Sieglinde grew to be a huge, silken, light brown animal —quiet, gentle, affectionate, always profoundly dignified, and she lived to a great old age. Sieglinde liked nothing better than to stretch on the floor at Helen Keller's feet while Helen read, watching the rhythm of Helen's left hand as she ran it over line after line of braille.

In those days Helen Keller read almost continuously about blindness, in order to write and lecture on it competently. Blindness, she found, has always existed, as far back as human records go, and no doubt farther back than that. In olden times the blind were treated with contempt; they wandered through the streets in rags, begging for coins, and often were abused and ridiculed. Now and again some charitable wealthy person, or perhaps a local church, would gather the blind beggars together and give them clean shelter and food. But abuse or charity was all the blind could expect. Hundreds of years passed before it occurred to anyone that they could be useful in any way. Yet, through the ages there were talented blind persons to prove how gifted the blind could be if given an opportunity. There were blind poets, blind musicians, blind wise men.

As mankind progressed in other ways, especially in science and medicine, knowledge of blindness increased, too. It had many causes, doctors began to realize: smallpox, scarlet fever, eye injuries that became infected, and just plain poverty and dirt. Sometimes the eyes of babies born to sick mothers became infected at birth and their sight was soon destroyed.

The care of the blind progressed very slowly. Not until 1749, when Diderot, a French writer, published an article on the ability of the blind to be educated, did people really begin to think of the subject to any great extent. After

Diderot another Frenchman, named Valentin Haüy, watched with growing horror and anger as the blind were hooted at in the streets and made to behave like clowns to entertain a crowd. He began to spend his free hours reading to the blind and trying to understand them. He read articles by such men as Diderot, and one day he observed the work of the Abbé de l'Épée, who was teaching some deaf-mute children a sign language that he had adapted for them—giving them a chance to "talk" to one another. If deaf-mutes could be educated, then why not the blind? Haüy himself was the son of a poor weaver, and he knew how precious his education was to him and how hard he had struggled to achieve it. How much more precious would it be to those whose handicap was blindness instead of poverty?

Haüy decided to experiment with teaching a blind child, and he began with large letters carved out of wood. The youngster progressed rapidly, and soon the student himself suggested to Haüy that they try raised printing on a page. With pages of raised, or embossed, printing that the boy could feel with his finger tips, he progressed still faster, and in a few months he was actually reading. From that first experiment Valentin Haüy dedicated himself to founding and operating a school for the blind. Instead of clowns, his students became choir singers and organists. Instead of beggars, they became industrial workers, printers, and weavers. He promoted the publishing of books in raised print for the blind, and he took his students about the country giving demonstrations. Before Haüy's life ended, he had roused public interest not only in France but in other countries as well. Schools for the blind began to open up all over Europe and in America, and more aids and devices were invented for them.

While Haüy was busy with his school in Paris, a three-year-old boy was watching his father fashion leather into a saddle in the French village of Coupvray. Suddenly an awl slipped from his father's hand and struck the boy in the eye. Not only did the boy lose the sight of that eye, but it became infected and the infection spread to the other eye. Because doctors did not understand infection in 1813, the boy became totally blind. The boy's name was Louis Braille.

Louis Braille's parents eventually took him to the Haüy school for the blind in Paris. The young student seemed slow and dull at first, but as he began to learn and understand language and all that could be done with it he developed into the most brilliant student who had ever come to the school. He was literary and gifted mechanically, and he had musical talent as well. He loved playing the organ and violoncello. By the time he had reached his teens, he knew that his life must concern itself with the problems of the blind, and one problem challenged him more than any other—how to help them to read better. One day he discovered that a code of raised dots had been invented as a military code, to be read on the battlefield at night without the use of light. Braille's imagination leaped ahead, and after a great deal of experimenting he finally devised the basic figure of six dots, the braille "cell," two dots wide and three high, out of which the whole alphabet is made. Today the word "braille" means the written language of the blind the world over.

Braille, Helen Keller thought! The braille that Anne Sullivan had taught her, and the braille slate she had learned to use as a child! She had taken these all for granted.

What of those, though, who were both deaf and blind? Unteachable, had been the universal opinion until so recently that Miss Keller felt a little chill when she realized how narrowly she had escaped that same opinion. Had she been born just a few years sooner, there would have been no stubborn, determined Anne Sullivan to teach her, no language at all, no communication with other human beings, no paper wings on which to soar. She would probably have been placed lovingly in some institution and "cared for."

"I owe my happiness to Samuel Gridley Howe," she realized.

Samuel Gridley Howe had been a very young social worker, just returned to Boston from Greece, where during their revolution he had been helping to distribute food to the starving. He learned that the state of Massachusetts was planning to start a school for the blind and that they wanted him to be its first director. Knowing very little of blindness, he returned to Europe for a year to observe in the schools there. At last in 1832 he was back in Boston beginning his great work at the brand-new school for the blind. He was so successful with his first students that enthusiam for the school spread rapidly; the state appropriated more money; Colonel Thomas H. Perkins donated a mansion to house it, and the school was renamed for him—the Perkins Institution for the Blind. (Today it is a private school and is called Perkins School for the Blind.)

Dr. Howe had been director of the Perkins Institution for about five years when the greatest challenge of his career was brought to him—a seven-year-old child who was both deaf and blind; her name was Laura Bridgman. As he looked at the little creature, he wondered how much he could do to make her into an understanding human being. No deaf-blind person had ever been educated before. He decided to try the impossible.

He began to work with Laura Bridgman, using words of raised letters and matching them to objects, until the miracle happened. Laura Bridgman's face lighted up with the understanding of words. Charles Dickens, on a trip to America a few years later, saw the educated Laura Bridgman. He wrote of it in *American Notes*, Helen Keller's mother read the book. Thus the chain reaction went on.

But Doctor Howe had not taught Laura to speak.

"The next task is mine," Helen Keller knew. "I must prove to the world that the deaf-blind can be taught speech."

Her own speech wasn't yet clear in spite of her constant practicing. When she appeared before an audience, she had to use an interpreter.

Even though she herself was deeply dissatisfied with her accomplishments, she was moving mountains just the same. Public interest in the affairs of the blind was rising: in

periodicals, in women's clubs, in civic groups. State legis-
latures were beginning to consider establishing schools for
them. In 1907 Mrs. William Ziegler, whose husband had
founded the Royal Baking Company, began the *Matilda
Ziegler Magazine,* a monthly in braille for the blind, and
Walter G. Holmes became its editor. About the same time
another important magazine, *Outlook for the Blind,* was
started by Mr. Charles F. F. Campbell, a professional
worker for the blind. It was in regular print and helped
workers for the blind to keep up-to-date on what was being accomplished.

Those who knew how much effect Helen Keller's influence was having never stopped encouraging her: Dr. Bell,
Mark Twain, Mr. Hitz, Mr. Wade, Mr. Holmes, Mr. Campbell. She had begun to correspond with Dr. James Kerr
Love, a surgeon in Glasgow, Scotland, and he added his
encouragement to the others.

Helen Keller was a miracle that people thronged to see
whenever she appeared anywhere. Police were often necessary to hold back the crowds that tried to close in around
her to touch her. People even invaded the privacy of the
Wrentham house, far more people than had the right to
do so. They came out of curiosity to ask bold questions.
They came seeking favors, even begging for money for
themselves or worthy causes, feeling that Helen Keller
must be as rich as she was famous.

Being a deeply sensitive person, she could not help becoming interested in a growing list of human concerns.
She tried to limit herself, but it was no use. One handicap
was often related to another. Why were so many babies

born blind? Not enough proper medical care at birth. Why not enough care? Often, the answer was poverty, or not enough hospitals and clinics. Why did so many adults lose their sight? Sometimes the conditions they worked under in factories ruined their eyes. Then there must be an end of slums, an end of poverty, an end of unhealthy working conditions, an end of all human misery.

In the fall of 1908 Helen Keller published her next book, *The World I Live In,* a collection of the articles she had written for *Century Magazine.*

She wanted to move on to new subjects, to grow in her art, but she found that the public wanted only to read about her. "There must be more you can tell us about yourself and your personal experiences," her editors said. Of course, there was, but there was more, much more, to write about. There was the wide, wide world, mankind, the universe.

One day Helen and Anne were both out in a nearby field, directing and helping the hired man as he built a stone wall along the edge of the property. As Helen caressed the rough surface of the field stones with her finger tips an idea began to come to her. Later in the day she sat down at her typewriter and started her long poem, *The Song of the Stone Wall.*

> *Come walk with me, and I will tell*
> *What I have read in this scroll of stone;*
> *I will spell out this writing on hill and meadow.*
> *It is a chronicle wrought by praying workmen,*

The forefathers of our nation—
Leagues upon leagues of sealed history awaiting an interpreter.
This is New England's tapestry of stone

.   .   .   .

With searching feet I walk beside the wall;
I plunge and stumble over the fallen stones;
I follow the windings of the wall
Over the heaving hill, down by the meadow-brook,
Beyond the scented fields, by the marsh where rushes grow.
On I trudge through pine woods fragrant and cool
And emerge amid clustered pools and by rolling acres of
    rye . . .

She toiled many hours a day for many weeks over the poem, and it was book-length when she finished it.

It did no good for John Macy or Anne to ask her to slacken a bit, but there were one or two people in the world who could persuade Helen Keller to leave her type-writer for a while and take a holiday, and Mark Twain was among them.

"I command you all three to come and spend a few days with me in 'Stormfield,'" he wrote, and Helen and the Macys accepted gladly.

"Stormfield" was a huge, roomy house that Mark Twain had built for himself in Redding, Connecticut. There he lived almost alone, since his wife had died and his only living daughter was married.

He was in his seventies in 1909, but Helen found him just as gay and witty and warm as the first time she had met him at Mrs. Laurence Hutton's. As they sat around his dinner table, he leaned back in his chair and told story after story, while Anne or John spelled them into her hand with the finger alphabet.

Away from the table, he held Helen's fingers to his lips whenever he wanted to talk to her. At bedtime he himself escorted Helen to her room.

"You'll find cigars in your night table," he told her jovially.

During the daytime he took her walking over the grounds, describing every shrub and tree to her that they passed.

Billiards had always been Mark Twain's favorite game, and one evening he completely ignored Miss Keller's handicaps and said, "Come. Let's go downstairs and have a game of billiards."

"Oh, Mr. Clemens," said Helen. "It takes sight to play billiards."

"Not the kind of billiards we play around here," he retorted. "The blind couldn't play worse."

Helen came home from "Stormfield" feeling refreshed and gay and filled with new energy.

There was so much to be done! All during the next year she worked hard, and yet she knew there was one great barrier to achieving all she wanted to achieve—her only real handicap—her inability to speak understandably. She fretted over it a great deal, but no solution seemed possible until at last she happened to meet Mr. Charles A. White, who was teaching singing at the Boston Conservatory of Music.

"I may be able to help you," he said. "I should certainly like to try."

Miss Keller thanked him, and gave his offer some thought.

"I think I should like to work with Mr. White," she said to the Macys soon after.

By the following winter it had been arranged. Mr. White came out to Wrentham each Saturday, gave Miss Keller her speech lesson, and returned to Boston on Sunday.

Helen Keller's heart sang as she began her exercises with him. Now, now! Now her only handicap was to be conquered! She would be able to stand on lecture platforms and speak without benefit of interpreter.

9 * I Stretch Out My Hands

Miss keller soon had to realize that, while Mr. White was a very gifted teacher, he was not a magician. He drilled her in vowels and consonants. He worked to teach her how to pitch her voice high and low. She had heard no human voice since her infancy, and so she had no idea how to modulate her own. She was speaking in a monotone way back in her throat. He worked to teach her rhythm and the way to accent words to make them lilt along. Lesson after lesson they labored together, and still she often produced sounds that were embarrassing to those who heard them.

"A hearing person speaks a language learned he knows not how," she said in despair.

She was living under an accumulation of tensions. Her speech lessons were nervewracking. Money was an ever-present problem, since the small annuity she received from Mr. Rogers wasn't enough, and magazines would purchase her articles only when they were about herself. On top of it all she was up to her chin in the campaign for woman suffrage that was working toward its highest pitch.

Her heart and soul were in that campaign. Women must have more freedom, more expression, more voice in the government. Helen even marched in parades behind banners declaring for "Votes for Women."

And there were other pressures. In fact, during the early 1900's Helen Keller's whole point of view was changing. She was just beginning to discover how much unnecessary misery and suffering there was in the world. She, who had grown up in a very sheltered way, protected by loved ones, was shocked by what she was learning.

"I want to see these things. I want to know about them."

She insisted on visiting slum areas and factories, especially with Mrs. Macy, because she knew she could trust her companion to describe scenes exactly as they were.

One day she read a book called *New Worlds for Old*, by H. G. Wells, and it clarified her thinking for the time being. She concluded that she was a socialist. She and the Macys had been having long conversations on socialism, since John Macy was already a member of the party. Anne Sullivan Macy disagreed with both her husband and Helen Keller. Their ideas were too extreme, she said; they expected too much.

But socialist meant social reform to Helen Keller. H. G. Wells talked of good will toward all men, and he said there ought to be some kind of planning to prevent poverty and slums, to provide clean and safe working conditions and limit the number of working hours. Mr. Wells was not a fanatic; he could see a lot of faults in socialism. He was an idealist, and socialism was idealistic. So was Helen Keller.

Today we have better planning than in those days. We have unions to arrange contracts between employers and employees. We have social security for the aged, housing projects, and free medical clinics. In fact, the one social problem arising out of poverty and slum conditions that disturbed Miss Keller most deeply—blindness in newborn babies—is a thing of the past in the United States. Today most babies are born in hospitals, and their eyes are treated immediately to protect them from infections that would destroy their sight.

But the subtlest pressure on Helen Keller in those days was a secret fear that had begun to creep into her heart—the fear of losing Anne Sullivan Macy. The day was bound to come when she would have to find another companion, because Mrs. Macy would not be able to stand the strain for many more years. Mrs. Macy was only forty-six, but her health and her eyesight were both failing.

Helen Keller was only thirty-two, filled with tremendous energy and drive and the will to accomplish as much as possible in every day, and whatever Helen Keller did her companion must also do. Helen was both dependent and extremely demanding, and to be her companion meant complete self-denial. From the day in 1887, twenty-five years before, when she had first arrived in Tuscumbia, Anne Sullivan had given her life to Helen Keller, because that was how she had wanted it to be.

When the doctor ordered Mrs. Macy to the hospital for a serious operation, Helen Keller was plunged into black despair. What was she without her companion? Helpless! She could not even remain in her own home, but must be taken to the home of friends to be *cared for*.

"I am a perpetual stumbling block, a handicap, a hindrance, a hanger-on. I am a tremendous burden to everyone."

It was a bitter and depressing experience and a frightening lesson as well. Helen realized that hers was a special kind of selfishness about which little could be done. When she and Anne were reunited at Wrentham a few weeks later, Helen had resolved to find someone else to relieve Anne at least part of the time. Anne Sullivan had made her own resolution: to recover.

"Mr. White says you can begin public speaking soon, and I am going to get back my strength so that I can go about with you."

Helen had been studying with Mr. White for nearly two years. She still could not speak without an interpreter, and she had begun to realize that she never would, but her speech had improved noticeably as a result of her work with him.

By the following winter Mrs. Macy had recovered sufficiently for a public appearance to be planned, and on February 6, 1913, the two women went to the auditorium of the Hillside School in Montclair, New Jersey, to speak on the subject, "The Heart and the Hand: or, The Right Use of the Senses."

To Helen an audience was a warm, damp cloud of human

breath and the odors of tobacco and cosmetics, and their applause was the vibration of the stage boards under her feet. In Montclair they were all waiting for her—the warmth and odors and the rush of vibrations when she appeared, but as she set foot on the platform her courage dissolved and she was stricken once more with an attack of stage fright. Her throat muscles locked, she lost control of her voice, and completely forgot everything Mr. White had taught her. But because she was a person of tremendous will power, she managed after a short pause to give her speech in some kind of voice. Then she fled from the platform in tears.

"A failure! A failure! A total failure! It is too difficult, too difficult; I cannot do the impossible."

"Audience nerves," Mr. White explained to her. "Something that every speaker and artist must cope with. The only way to overcome it is by continuously appearing before audiences."

He simply would not let her give up. About two weeks later she appeared as one of the guest speakers at the opening of the new building of The Lighthouse on East 59th Street in New York City. As leaders of the different churches and various organizations for the blind gathered on the platform, Helen Keller, sitting beside Anne Sullivan Macy, felt far more at ease than she had in Montclair. They were all waiting for the principal speaker, the President of the United States, William Howard Taft. Soon the chairman came to Helen Keller and said, "Miss Keller, the President will be late, and I am going to seat you in his chair."

She laughed gayly and replied, "I am the first woman to be President of the United States."

When Anne finally signaled her to rise and give her talk, she found it much easier to remember Mr. White's teaching.

The fact that she was speaking for so splendid a project as The Lighthouse gave her self-confidence, too.

The first Lighthouse for the blind had been started in 1905 by Miss Winifred Holt, daughter of the publisher, Henry Holt. Miss Holt had consulted many experts in the field as a first step, and when Helen Keller received Miss Holt's letter she wrote back without a minute's hesitation to say, "The burden of the blind is not blindness, but idleness."

And so Miss Holt went ahead to found a social and recreational center where the blind could have a real community, a library, a swimming pool, bowling alleys, a museum, table games, parties, as well as classes in sewing, needlework, weaving, and other crafts. Today there are Lighthouses all over the world.

After the ceremony at the opening of the Lighthouse building, Helen Keller completed the reading of proofs for her latest book, *Out of the Dark*, another collection of her articles.

Then a major decision had to be made, one to summon all the courage and stubbornness that Helen Keller had ever possessed: the decision to go on her first lecture tour. She knew audiences and audience nerves, stages and stage fright. She knew that ahead of her was a continuous experience in these things, and a parade of strange hotel rooms to find her way around in, strange hands to clasp, strange odors that she couldn't remain with long enough to identify.

Anne was to travel with her, and Helen did not ask, "What about John?" She knew that the Macys had decided to separate. They had been slowly drifting apart during the last several years because of different temperaments, different tastes and ambitions. That spring John Macy went on a long trip to Europe, and Anne and Helen set out to visit a list of American cities.

At each program, Helen Keller and Anne Sullivan Macy appeared on the platform together. Mrs. Macy spoke first, explaining deaf-blindness, the teaching of the deaf-blind, and the importance of teaching speech to the deaf-blind. After that she told something of Helen Keller's personal history, and then she signaled Helen to stand beside her. Together they gave a demonstration of how they conversed. Helen read Anne's lips with her finger tips and spoke to the audience herself. Helen thrilled people. She was the big attraction they had come to see. They loved and adored her. But the fact remained, that they couldn't really understand her. Oh, now and then a phrase or a sentence, yes; but most of what she said had to be restated by Mrs. Macy. They loved her anyway. They applauded her courage and determination and dedication.

Mrs. Keller had come from Alabama to be with them as they traveled and lectured all during the winter of 1913–1914, to the West Coast and back. She helped with the multitude of details: hotel reservations, meals, train tickets, baggage, porters, appointments. Helen Keller was public property as far as the public was concerned, and people everywhere boldly sought her out, asking favors, taking up her time and energy, plaguing her with personal questions. Mrs. Keller and Mrs. Macy had their hands full.

When they finally returned to Wrentham in the spring, all three of them were ready to collapse. Mrs. Keller was no longer young enough for such an ordeal, and Helen wondered where the money would come from to pay someone else to do what her mother had been doing.

And Anne's health? Anything that overtaxed Anne helped to shorten her service as an indispensable companion. Helen Keller reflected upon a conversation she had had a year or two earlier with a very great man and his wife, Mr. and Mrs. Andrew Carnegie. At the time, he had wanted to arrange an annual income for her, and she had refused out of sheer pride. She so earnestly wanted to earn her own way—and Anne's!

The Carnegies made the offer to her more than once.

"Think the matter over for a while," Mr. Carnegie had said. "You can have it whenever you want it."

Well, she had thought the matter over. She went to her typewriter and wrote Mr. Carnegie a humble note of acceptance. She received her first check in a day or two, together with a loving and generous letter.

And now to find Anne an assistant! But where and who?

One autumn day in 1914 a sturdy young woman with a strong Scottish burr applied for the job.

Had she been in America long? they asked.

No, she replied. She had come to America because she heard it was a land of opportunity.

Did she know the finger alphabet?

No.

Had she had any experience in working with the handicaps of deafness and blindness?

No, never.

But she must realize that this was no ordinary secretarial post. All kinds of other duties would crowd in upon her day.

That was all right, Miss Polly Thomson assured Miss Keller and Mrs. Macy.

What other talents did she have beside her secretarial training?

She could, she assured everyone, sew, cook, make a household run smoothly, and be courteous to strangers.

Had Polly Thomson been dropped straight out of heaven into the Wrentham living room, she could not have been a greater blessing. There were times in the years that followed when Helen thought she really had come from heaven rather than from Scotland. Everything was less difficult with Polly around: dogs, bank balances, callers, lecture tours.

The lecture tour of 1914–1915 was very different from the previous season's, because world events changed it. World War I had begun in Europe, and wherever Helen and her party went the air, the newspapers, conversations, were full of war talk.

War to Helen was one more unnecessary misery that man

inflicted on himself. It horrified and shocked her. This was not the first time she had thought of war, nor the first war to affect her life. Her father had fought in the Civil War, and she herself could remember the Boer War in South Africa and the Spanish-American War. The present war was bigger still, and it felt much closer than the others.

Peace! World peace! If there was to be good will to all men, if there was to be an end of poverty and injustice, then there must be peace in which to achieve these ideals. Swedenborg taught that God is Love, Wisdom, and Power. War, then, was godlessness. So, to her campaigning for the blind, for woman suffrage, and for social reforms, Helen Keller added pacifism. When she went on a lecture tour, it was to speak for peace and disarmament.

Strong or extreme opinions always stir up opposition. Many of Miss Keller's closest and dearest friends had scolded and reasoned with her about her socialism; now there were more to scold her for her pacifism.

"Oh, the pacifists are just using her for publicity!" some said, since every opinion that Miss Keller expressed was reported in the newspapers.

But pacifism was her own free decision.

When she read that Jane Addams, founder of Hull House in Chicago, was appealing to everyone to send peace messages to President Woodrow Wilson, Helen Keller promptly sent him a telegram of her own:

> I beseech you to help stop this war. We know that you believe in justice, mercy, and the brotherhood of man. We are convinced that it is in your power, as the head of the

nation, to take the first step toward peace negotiations. We urge a conference of neutral nations dedicated to finding a just settlement of the war. . . .

With so much activity the winter passed very quickly indeed, and when summer arrived again she could scarcely believe that Polly Thomson had been with her a whole year.

"We must plan to do without Polly while she is on vacation!"

Furthermore, the doctor had ordered Mrs. Macy to take a rest, and they must plan to do without her as well.

Polly returned to Scotland for a few weeks, Mrs. Macy went to Lake Placid, and Mrs. Keller came to Wrentham to look after her daughter's personal needs. A young man named Peter Fagan joined the household as Helen Keller's temporary secretary.

Mr. Fagan had been a newspaper reporter. He was well-read, brilliant, and interesting. During the summer months he and Helen became close friends, and he stayed on during the late autumn.

"You are feeling despondent," he said to her one evening.

Yes, she was. He had learned to read her moods. She had allowed herself to become depressed at the thought of doing without her beloved teacher.

He took hold of her hand.

"Has anyone ever told you that you are a very beautiful woman?"

Beautiful? She? No, no one had. She had no way of knowing it herself. There were no mirrors in her life. She liked to dress stylishly and have her hair groomed carefully by one companion or another, but she hadn't known . . .

Had she ever thought of marriage? he asked.

Long ago Dr. Bell had talked to her of love and marriage, and now as she sat with Peter Fagan he was proposing marriage. He would always be with her, he promised, to read to her, to travel with her and interpret for her. She need never again suffer the deep fear of being left alone.

Dr. Bell had advised her not to resist happiness, and she felt herself consenting. This would be a real and lasting union. Her fear and despondency vanished.

"We must tell everyone! The whole world must know!" she declared joyfully.

"Better wait a bit," Peter Fagan cautioned. "Your family and Teacher will probably disapprove at first. Let us keep our love secret a little while. Teacher is too ill to be excited just now, and we must tell her first."

They went on long walks together and talked of their future, until at length Helen grew uncomfortable about the deception, and so did Peter.

One evening as he brought her back to the house, she said, "Tomorrow I am going to tell Teacher. I can't keep it from her any longer."

But the newspapers exploded in the Keller household next morning like a bomb, even before Helen was out of bed. They were full of gossip about Miss Keller's engagement to Mr. Fagan. An extra sharp reporter had found their application for a marriage license in the Boston City

Hall, and there was no disputing it, because it was in their two handwritings, one the square-lettered writing of a blind person.

Mrs. Keller realized that Peter Fagan was not quite so altruistic, nor so talented, as Helen thought, and she realized, too, that Helen was seeking a substitute for Mrs. Macy. When she demanded that her daughter explain what had been going on, Helen in a panic denied everything. No, no! There was nothing, no engagement, no license. When Teacher hurried to her room to investigate the rumpus, Helen lied about the whole thing again.

Mother Keller marched off to Mr. Fagan's room and ordered him to leave the house. Flushed with embarrassment, he obeyed, all the while supporting Helen's story. There was nothing; they had never applied for a marriage license, even though the Boston city records said otherwise. He took a Savannah Line steamer to Tampa, Florida, writing to Helen in braille to let her know where he was going.

Peter and Helen corresponded for a while, but they were so far apart, and privacy was so nearly impossible, that their romance gradually came to an end. Helen found herself living in a house full of heartbreak. She had never lied to Teacher before, had never caused unhappiness to others.

"Polly will take Miss Anne away for a rest," Mrs. Keller told her deaf-blind daughter, "and I intend to take you down to Montgomery. We will stay with Mildred and her husband [Warren Tyson] until everyone has recovered from the shock."

The shattered love affair seemed to mark a turning point in Helen Keller's life. When she and Anne and Polly were once more united they took stock of their situation. The Wrentham house was the scene of Anne's unhappy marriage and of Helen's upsetting romance, and it was too costly and too accessible. Anyone who took it into his head to do so could come knocking at the door.

"We need a less expensive place, and we need more privacy," they agreed.

So they sold the Wrentham house to the Jordan Marsh Company of Boston who converted it into a rest home. Helen, Anne, Polly, and Sieglinde soon found themselves a smaller house in Forest Hills on Long Island, a rather out-of-the-way place then, not at all built up as it is today.

Monthly checks still reached them from Mr. Carnegie and Mr. Rogers. But prices were rising so rapidly because of the war that the amounts were not nearly enough to run a household, particularly one where two persons were severely handicapped. Helen knew that the responsibility of earning money was hers. She and Anne could not get along without Polly, and Anne would never be really well again.

"I must find a way to earn enough money for all of us," Helen Keller determined. "It is my turn to take care of Teacher."

10 ∗ Hollywood and the Stage

THE PROBLEM OF earning money was something that almost everyone had to cope with and something that almost everyone was able to solve. But first, there were walls to be papered, woodwork to be painted, minor repairs to be made.

"As soon as we are settled in our new house, I'm sure I shall have some ideas about earning money," Helen decided.

Her prediction came true. Just a few weeks after they had moved in, an exciting suggestion arrived in the mail: a letter with a California postmark from Francis Trevelyan Miller, the author, who had made a name for himself as a historian of the Civil War.

"I am writing a history of the world," his letter said, in effect, "and a tremendous idea has occurred to me in the process of doing it. Have you ever thought of making a motion picture of your life? You could surely reach millions of people with your message about blindness through that medium. While so many people are thinking of destruction and war, what a happy blessing it would be to be able to show them ways to make the world a better place to live in!"

The movies! People made fabulous fortunes in the movies! This was the answer to her financial problems forever. If she made a movie of her life, she would have a lump sum of cash to invest, and she and Teacher and Polly could live on the income from their investments. At the same time— as Dr. Miller pointed out—it was a tremendous opportunity to get her message across to thousands of people who did not go to lectures.

The Forest Hills house became a beehive of conferences, phone calls, correspondence, with a long list of Helen Keller's extraordinary friends. Helen typed out letter after letter. How was the film to be financed? Should they solicit donations? No, no, that wasn't practical.

"I shall finance it," one of her wealthy admirers came forward and said.

"Oh, then, I shall be able at the same time to tell the world what a generous man you are!"

"No; I don't want you to tell anyone. My name must be left out of it."

She had to consent if she wanted the money.

At last arrangements were made with the Brunton Studio in Hollywood and with the Director, Mr. George Foster Platt. Dr. Miller was to write the scenario.

Like excited young girls going to Hollywood for their first screen test, the three women set out across the continent once more, to put in the most strenuous six months they had ever experienced.

"My voice won't matter this time," Helen said again and again on the train going out. Those were the days of silent pictures.

Hollywood proved to be a vibrant place, a place filled with artifice and unreality, where stone walls felt like pasteboard and snowflakes did not melt. Helen felt hands filled with nervous tension and changeable temperament, and she smelled all sorts of new odors: celluloid, grease paint, fireproofing, canvas.

Eagerly they sat down in conference with the story experts. But the experts shook their heads when they examined the material. There wasn't any picture in Helen Keller's life. Why, there wasn't even a love story! Helen and Anne sat tightlipped and did not mention Peter Fagan.

"If you will let us fictionize a bit . . ."

"No!" declared Anne Sullivan Macy.

"No!" echoed Helen Keller as soon as the query was relayed to her. "I want a true account of my life."

At last, after a series of conferences and discussions, some of them rather heated and strained, the framework of a story began to take shape. The picture was to be called *Deliverance* since Helen Keller had been delivered from her physical handicaps by knowledge, and from her mental handicaps by her new social and religious beliefs. The story was in three parts. Part one was her childhood, with Edna Ross playing Helen Keller. Part two was her young girlhood and her valiant effort to learn to speak, and here Ann

Mason played the lead. In part three Helen Keller was to play herself.

When the time came to shoot the third part, Helen Keller breathed a sigh of thanks for Director Platt. She felt clumsy, awkward, camera-shy, and self-conscious. Director Platt usually stood behind the camera with a megaphone in his hand shouting directions to the performers, but for Helen Keller he arranged a special code. He stamped on the floor and she could feel the vibrations through her feet. One stamp meant move in one direction, two stamps meant move in another direction, and so on.

Before he began shooting a scene he described it carefully to Mrs. Macy who spelled it into Helen's hand. Then Helen moved out upon the set to act out her own self dramatically. The floor vibrated; she turned; it vibrated; she turned again. The scene was cut; she must go back and do it over. She was sure she had never done anything worse in her life, even though those who watched her on the set called her a "born actress" and a "real trooper."

The big finale of the picture would seem rather amateurish to us today, but it was the fashion in those days. Helen Keller, dressed in a flowing gown, holding a trumpet to her lips, mounted on a great white horse, rode along ahead of a huge crowd of extras. Helen Keller leading mankind to its *deliverance!*

The picture was finished at last. A weary but hopeful trio of women returned to Forest Hills in December of 1918. Their future was secure, and the world was at peace once more. They asked no more.

"With income from our future investments I shall be able to devote myself heart and soul to the affairs of the blind," declared Helen Keller. "Oh, there is so much yet to be done for them. The public must be educated to understand and appreciate them. The adult blind must be trained in trades and skills so that they can become self-supporting and self-respecting. The different kinds of braille must be standardized into one system. All kinds of research are needed on their problems. Industrial accidents must be prevented. Teaching methods must be continually improved. We need a clearinghouse for all these efforts. There are groups all over the country working for the blind without referring to one another. They are often duplicating their efforts. Thank heaven for financial freedom to work for mankind!"

It was not hard at that point to imagine the Forest Hills house floating gently in space on a fluffy pink cloud.

There were a few months to wait before the picture was ready for its debut, and meanwhile Helen Keller and Anne Sullivan Macy journeyed to Baltimore, Maryland, to visit blind soldiers in the U.S. General Hospital there. Oh, Helen Keller knew she was going to have plenty to say about blindness caused by war!

As they entered the ward, Helen felt Anne pause and shudder. They knew and understood each other, these two. All they needed was a touch to convey a thought. Helen felt Anne's horror.

"Describe it to me!" she insisted. "Tell me what you see."

Anne did. Most of the men had other injuries in addition to their blindness—shattered or lost limbs, shock, body wounds.

Helen Keller moved forward into the ward. In one bed she found a man raging with anger about his loss of sight.

"I once raged with anger," she told him as she held his hand. "I was rebelling against my handicap."

The kinship that he felt for her made him feel calmer.

She found another in the depths of despair, because he was trying to learn braille, but his fingers were too coarsened by manual labor.

"The braille dots only feel like sandpaper to me," he told her.

"Your hands will grow softer and more sensitive with time," she promised him.

Most important of all, they knew who Helen Keller was, and the thrill of having her come right to their bedside was a tonic for them. They felt her hands and found them loving; they felt her face and found it smiling.

And so back to New York and the grand opening of *Deliverance*, at the Lyric Theatre in New York City on August 18, 1919. The theatre was full. The audience liked the film. When the point of the story arrived where Helen Keller finally appeared to say, "I am not dumb now," the audience burst into enthusiastic applause. The reviews next day were good. And that was practically the end of the story. *Deliverance* was an artistic triumph and a financial failure, and those who made it never received any profits. It just didn't click, as so often happens in show business.

The pink cloud vanished from Forest Hills and the house settled down upon its foundation.

During the next few weeks Helen Keller had to exert a great deal of self-discipline to prevent herself from sinking deep into despondency. Her faith was being tested. She herself had once written, "I believe in God; I believe in man; I believe in the power of the spirit." Well, she still believed these three things, and she must go on believing them.

When Helen had about reached her lowest point, spiritually and financially, Mrs. Macy came to her and spelled into her hand, "Someone is at the door."

Mrs. Macy left and returned a few minutes later to present Mr. Harry Weber.

Helen Keller reached up and placed her finger tips on his lips while he explained his visit.

"I am a theatrical agent," he said. "I saw your motion picture *Deliverance*, and I want to put you on the stage."

Miss Keller laughed. "Are you going to make me rich?" she asked.

"It's a gamble," he told her, "but I think a vaudeville act with you as the principal would go over big."

"We thought a motion picture with me as the principal would go over, too. Now we know better."

At long last Mr. Weber was able to persuade Miss Keller, Mrs. Macy, and Miss Thomson to go on the road with a short act, even though he could not persuade them to believe it would ever be a resounding success. No pink clouds this time!

The act was to be a dignified affair, something like the lectures, with signature music added. Mrs. Macy appeared first, followed by Miss Keller, who found her way out onto the stage unescorted. There was a clever arrangement of draperies, furniture, and flowers to guide her.

"We must begin modestly," Helen insisted.

"Yes," Mr. Weber promised. "I am going to try out the act in Mount Vernon, New York, before I risk it in the city."

The famous vaudeville actress, Sophie Tucker, taught them how to put on make-up.

On the sixteenth of February, 1920, Helen Keller stood behind the heavy stage draperies waiting for her cue from Polly. The signal came, she moved the curtain back with one hand, and stepped forward. Applause vibrated through the boards under her feet, and she experienced a horrible moment of stage fright, panic, a dry-as-dust throat. In another second, though, the determined little girl, who had once said she must learn everything, took over, and Helen Keller moved out onto the stage to stand beside her teacher.

She felt once more the damp warmth of the breath, the odors of tobacco and perfumes, and she sensed a response of surprise and joy when she actually spoke. She knew at once that a vaudeville audience was much friendlier than a lecture audience, much more loving and generous. A wave of happiness engulfed her as she stood before the people of Mount Vernon.

She played for a whole week in Mount Vernon, and

then she went to the Palace Theatre in New York City. New York audiences loved her without reservation, and she was held over for a second week. Triumphantly, Mr. Weber began to make long-range plans.

"We'll stay in the East this season," he told her, "and next winter I am going to book you on the Orpheum Circuit, coast to coast."

Thus, Helen Keller became a high-paid prima donna, playing to packed houses all over the United States and Canada for four years.

11 * The American Foundation for the Blind

ANNE SULLIVAN MACY was able to appear in the act with Helen Keller for only about a year. The physical strain proved too much, and the glaring footlights tormented her eyes. But she continued to travel with Helen, and Polly took her place in the act.

There were other changes and events on the public scene and in her private life that occurred during the four years that Helen Keller spent upon the vaudeville stage. Shortly after her triumphant beginning, the nineteenth amendment was added to the Constitution giving women citizens of the United States the right to vote.

During the winter of 1921–1922, when she was playing in Los Angeles, Anne came to her dressing room and laid a hand gently on her shoulder. That communicating touch made Helen ask at once, was there news? Yes. Bad news? Yes. Well, Helen was ready to hear it.

It was her mother, Anne told her. Mrs. Arthur Keller had died suddenly at Mildred's home in Montgomery.

Helen sat very still for a moment trying to grasp what had just been said to her. Her mother had not been ill! Or had she? No, said Anne; Mrs. Keller had gone quickly and without suffering.

That same spring, when Helen Keller was appearing in Chicago, Carl Sandburg, the poet, was in the audience, but she did not know about it for a long time afterward. Eventually she received a note from him, confessing that he had been so thrilled by her performance that he had rushed home and written her a glowing fan letter. But his courage failed him for a while, and he could not bring himself to mail it. "Possibly the finest thing about your performance," he told her, "is that those who hear and see you feel that zest for living, the zest that you radiate. . . ."

The event that made her happiest during those four years of vaudeville was the beginning of the American Foundation for the Blind. It came into existence in Vinton, Iowa, at the 1921 annual meeting of the American Association of Workers for the Blind.

A national agency at last! A clearinghouse for all the scattered efforts that were being made for the blind! This group had been needed for a long time. Until the AFB came into being, the only national group had been a National Committee that devoted itself to the task of preventing blindness.

Helen Keller read the news with satisfaction. The AFB was going to make a complete study of what was being done so that the whole field could be coordinated. It was going to launch a systematic research program to determine the best ways of helping the blind.

"Now there will be tremendous progress. We will make great strides."

The idea of establishing a national agency had been thought of many times by workers for the blind during the preceding twenty years. Charles F. F. Campbell had probably been the first to think of it, and he was certainly the first to do anything about it when he started his technical magazine for professional workers, *Outlook for the Blind*. In 1921 the blind H. Randolph Latimer, President of the American Association and Superintendent of the Western Pennsylvania Institute for the Blind, decided to put the idea into action at the annual meeting of the American Association in Iowa. Major M. C. Migel became the first president of the AFB and contributed a large amount of money to finance its early days. Major Migel was a silk manufacturer by trade and head of the New York State Commission for the Blind. Dr. Robert Irwin became the first head of the research division of the AFB.

Helen Keller and Anne Sullivan Macy followed the beginnings of the AFB with keen interest, and when they returned to Forest Hills one summer they were not surprised to receive a telephone call from Major Migel's secretary.

"What does he want?" asked Helen.

"He wants you to work on a big fund-raising campaign for the AFB," Polly told her.

"And what did you tell him?"

"That you don't have the time now because you are planning to go on another vaudeville tour."

"And?"

"His secretary nearly died of shock!"

The room was suddenly filled with laughter. Many people were horrified at the idea of an eminent person like Miss Keller going into vaudeville. Her retort always was, "Well, what do *you* think I should do for a living?" That usually silenced the comments.

At the end of her fourth year in vaudeville, the AFB approached her once more to join its staff. The salary it was able to offer her was much smaller than her vaudeville salary, naturally, but it was adequate, and in the back of her mind was the gnawing realization that Anne needed a respite from strenuous traveling. "Helen has a mind of her own," her father had said when she was only six months old, and at forty-four she had more of a mind of her own than ever.

She soon announced her decision: "I shall discontinue vaudeville and join the staff of the AFB."

Harry Weber almost cried when he heard the bad news, but when Helen explained her situation to him he accepted it. She had a special responsibility in life. Long ago she had dedicated herself to the cause of those who suffered from loss of sight. Her vaudeville appearances had aroused tremendous public interest in the subject of blindness. Now she must do the next task: route that public interest toward the organization best able to plan help for the blind. She was going on the road to raise funds for the American Foundation for the Blind.

But alone with Anne later she suddenly quailed as she realized what she was about to do. She was going begging. She was going to appear in the role of blind beggar.

"Oh, Teacher!" she said, holding tightly to Anne's hand. "I don't want to do this. It is too humiliating. For years we have worked to save the blind from lives as beggars, and now we must do it ourselves."

"This is begging to end begging," said Anne both to Helen and herself.

"I still do not speak distinctly."

"No; but you have made steady progress. Helen, you are the only living person who can convince the world that handicaps like yours can be overcome, that the handicapped may live dignified, useful lives."

Helen Keller was experiencing only a moment of wavering. She and Teacher both knew she had no intention of backing down. They had never ceased to work together on voice drills and exercises, because whether she was making a silent movie, appearing in vaudeville, or fund-raising for the blind, there was always a further important message implied in her public speaking: *the deaf and the deaf-blind can and must be taught to speak.*

Helen Keller still clung to her dream that some day she would stand on a platform alone, without an interpreter, and speak to her audience, knowing that every word she uttered would be understood.

Her crippled speech didn't matter to the public the way

it did to her. She had an electrifying effect wherever she went, and when she set out on her fund-raising campaign for the AFB—goal: one million dollars—she melted hearts by the scores. She invaded New York City's sacred financial world and captured the interest of Felix Warburg and Otto H. Kahn, of Kuhn, Loeb and Company. Mr. Warburg had been supporting the Henry Street Settlement, help for juvenile offenders, hospitals, European famine relief, and the YMHA for years; and Mr. Kahn was just as noted for his generosity.

When Helen Keller reached Chicago she won a generous donation from Carrie Jacobs Bond, the composer who wrote "I Love You Truly" and "A Perfect Day." In Detroit Mr. and Mrs. Henry Ford and Edsel Ford each gave her a large donation. The elder Mr. Ford, she learned, was employing seventy-three blind men in his automobile plants. He had found that their sensitive hands did excellent precision work. No pity in that, Helen Keller realized joyfully. The greatest task of helping the blind was re-educating the public, and that was one of the tasks the AFB was going to do.

Dear reader [she wrote on this point later in her memoirs], let me ask you to stop for a moment and try to visualize your blind neighbor. You have met him often in the the street, in sunshine and in rain, cautiously threading his way among his unseen fellows, his cane tapping the pavement, his body tense, his ears straining to hear sounds that will guide him in the invisible maze. You have glanced at him pityingly, and gone your way thinking how strange his thoughts must be, his feelings how different from your own. My friend, have done with this cruel illusion and try to learn the truth. Hearts are hearts and pain is pain, and joy, ambition, and love are in the blind man even as in you. He wants the same things that you do. Like you he dreams of love and success and happiness. You would still be yourself if an accident blinded you tomorrow; your desires would be the same.

Helen Keller's campaign for the AFB lasted more than two years. She met Luther Burbank in Santa Rosa, California, and examined the new species of flowers and fruits that he was creating. John D. Rockefeller, Jr., gave her one of her largest donations. Mr. Rockefeller hated ignorance. In Hollywood Mary Pickford and her husband Douglas Fairbanks took her under their wing and used their influence to help her cause. The Ziegler family were their usual generous selves. The *Matilda Ziegler Magazine* for the blind was still growing in circulation, and Walter G. Holmes was still its editor.

Her fund-raising work caught on and grew like a happy contagion, fed by her popularity. School children began collecting nickels and dimes and mailing them to her, and churches of every denomination were running benefits. No wonder the AFB had wanted her to take to the road for them.

Those two years were strenuous, and the summers at the end of each season were a blessed relief. Summers were a time for more than rest; they were a time to reflect, ponder, evaluate, review. Helen Keller felt herself moving forward with such drive, felt such a sense of accomplishment when she thought of the year she had just completed, that she could almost forget her own handicaps in the satisfaction she felt in working for others. She knew there was great hope for the future of all handicapped persons, and that was what carried her on. Hope was the key to happiness—for the blind, the deaf, the deaf-blind. The only handicaps that could really defeat a human being were hopelessness and despair.

Time and again Anne Sullivan bolstered Helen's belief and hope with her own, saying it a little differently perhaps, but saying essentially the same thing.

Anne Sullivan was older—and ill.

She will go out of my life, Helen knew. Her life will probably end long before my own.

There was always a corner of Helen's mind reserved for Anne Sullivan Macy's health. Teacher was ill. Teacher was working beyond her strength. After the second year of fund-raising both Helen and Anne knew that Anne must remain at home from then on. No more traveling!

Helen Keller continued as a permanent staff member of the AFB, and in 1926 she and Polly journeyed to the national capital to enlist the interest of Congress and President Calvin Coolidge in the need for a national library for the blind.

"You will find President Coolidge rather cold," she had been told, but when she grasped his hand she felt warmth and comfort.

"I am greatly interested in your work," he told her, "and I will cooperate with you in every way possible."

The automatic response she received from Congressmen was, "If Helen Keller wants it, we are for it."

It was not long before the annual appropriation was made and the work of producing books for the blind had begun on a national scale.

And so home to Forest Hills once more and another spell of rest and quiet, with Polly shouldering the greatest burdens. Each morning Polly read Helen the newspapers, and after breakfast Helen went to her typewriter to answer her day's mail—again with Polly's help.

The publishing firm of Doubleday wanted Helen Keller to write a book that would bring the story of her life up to date, but Helen had already embarked on another book that must be finished first. It was to be called *My Religion* and was to be published by the Swedenborg Foundation.

In spite of rapidly failing eyesight, Anne Macy insisted on working on *My Religion* with her. A continuous competition went on between the two women: Helen finding ways and means to divert Anne from work, Anne trying to prevent Helen from realizing how bad her eyes really were.

My Religion came out in October, 1927, and Helen Keller had already begun to write *Midstream*, the sequel to *The Story of My Life*. Anne tried to work with her, but Helen refused to be deceived any longer.

"I cannot continue with the book," she told Mr. Frank Doubleday, and she explained the exact situation to him.

Midstream was an important book, and so he found a solution right away. He detailed one of his staff members,

Miss Nella Braddy, to assist Miss Keller. Nella Braddy (later Mrs. Keith Henney) proved an excellent choice. Her personality fitted into the household easily, and she became the reading eyes for the almost blind Mrs. Macy and the deaf-blind Miss Keller. *Midstream* was published two years later.

By that time Helen and Anne had at last reached a point of real relaxation in their lives, and in the summer of 1929 Helen beguiled Anne Macy into taking a vacation with her in the Adirondack Mountains in a quiet cottage on Long Lake, New York. Anne had insisted on an operation on her right eye recently, even though the doctor had told her it would be useless, and Helen wanted Anne to have a slow, pleasant recovery.

Since the day when she had first begun to fear losing her beloved teacher, Helen had known she must accept the idea, and as they settled themselves in their cottage she realized that they would not spend many more vacations together. She was acutely aware of it when she went swimming. She felt her way along her rope walk down to the water's edge and into the lake, and as the cold water swirled around her ankles a chill seized her heart. Anne Sullivan could no longer go swimming with her. Here, on this quiet summer day, in this peaceful place, she was going on alone without her lifelong companion.

A short while later she discovered that the same thought had occurred to Anne, for her teacher said, "Oh, Helen, what a sad experience it is to feel one's decline!"

In the autumn they returned to Forest Hills and their

work for the AFB. but they still lived in an atmosphere of relaxation. There were occasional afternoons when they could enjoy long conversations on anything in the world: religion, politics, social problems. Anne still did not accept the teachings of Swedenborg, even though she knew how much strength Helen derived from them. In politics neither of them was as radical as she had once been.

"I am mellowing," Helen Keller said one day as they sat together chatting. "I realize now that H. G. Wells made everything much too simple, but I still dream of an ideal world where there will be no handicap untended and no poverty."

"I would not be going blind if there were no poverty," said Anne.

"You never told me that. You told me only of your happy days with your younger sister and brother in Massachusetts and your father's Irish folklore."

"I was your teacher. I came into your life to make you happier, not to impose my private griefs on you."

"We are both middle-aged now," Helen prodded. "Tell me the whole story."

What Anne told her proved more shocking than Helen could possibly have imagined. Anne Sullivan's parents had been young Irish immigrants who had come to America, land of promise and plenty, to escape from a desperate famine in Ireland. They had found themselves as badly off as ever and in a foreign land. They settled in the village of Feeding Hills outside Springfield because other Irish families were there. Anne's father was an uneducated laborer, and that kind of help was plentiful. He was un-employed most of the time and missing from home a great deal. Anne was the first child to be born, and later there was another girl, Ellen, and a boy, Jimmie. Anne's mother developed tuberculosis and became too ill to care for the household. Neighbors did what they could for the impoverished Sullivans, but there were many in the same predicament. Anne's eyes developed the telltale red rims and granulations of trachoma, an eye infection. In the midst of the ever-worsening poverty, Ellen died of some sort of fever and lack of care, and shortly after that Mrs. Sullivan died. By the time Jimmie was five he was on crutches because of tuberculosis of the hip, and eight-year-old Anne was already half blind. But their situation did not go entirely unnoticed. Eventually friends gathered up the two neglected children and placed them in the poor-house in Tewksbury.

Helen Keller sat almost without breathing as Anne spelled the story into her hand.

The poorhouse was as poverty stricken as the children it was trying to care for. It was crowded and unsanitary. At least, though, she and Jimmie were allowed to remain together. Jimmie died before very much longer, and she was left completely alone—and blind.

"You came to me from Perkins Institution," said Helen.

"Perkins was only some twenty-odd miles away, but I was fourteen before I found my way into it."

"The year I was born."

"Yes. In the meantime this doctor or that tried to restore my sight, but without success. I was Irish and a fighter, and the atmosphere at Tewksbury had made a wild, bold little thing of me. I seethed and raged and secretly plotted to escape from the horrid place someday. Meanwhile, right-thinking people were beginning to be stirred about the conditions at Tewksbury, and eventually there was a public investigation. I knew the investigation was coming and that it was my chance of escape. Mr. Franklin Sanborn was the man in charge of it. When word got around that the investigators had arrived, I groped my way along the corridor until I heard a group talking, and one of them had a strange voice. I threw myself at him crying, 'Mr. Sanborn, Mr. Sanborn, I want to go to school!' "

"And you were rescued."

"Very soon after that I was transferred to Perkins. After I had been at Perkins about a year, a boarder in a house where I had a summer job suggested the Massachusetts Eye and Ear Infirmary. There a doctor performed an operation on each of my eyes and restored my sight."

Helen sat still for a long time before she asked, "What was the most difficult moment?"

"The death of my brother Jimmie, because I loved him so much and he was all I had. Losing him made me feel alone, utterly alone."

Helen asked no more questions. She knew there was one more book she must write—Teacher's story. Carelessly, selfishly, in writing *The Story of My Life* and *Midstream* she had told only of her own achievement, as though she had done it alone. Oh, yes, Anne had insisted on being left out, but she ought not to have listened. Helen Keller's achievement was Anne's.

Another resolve developed in Helen Keller's mind at the same time, one that she was going to put into effect immediately. Anne's last years were going to be as happy and restful as possible. She began to plan. There was one thing that she and Anne were definitely going to do together, something they had often talked about, something that Helen herself had prattled about since childhood. They were going to take a trip to Europe.

"Oh, no!" declared Anne when Helen finally mentioned it to her.

But Helen had everyone on her side.

"I shall write to my sister," said Polly Thomson. "She will find a cottage for us somewhere. You know, Cornwall is beautiful in the spring."

"Don't you want to see Ireland just once?" Nella Braddy added.

"I don't think I do," said Anne.

Word soon came that the AFB was happy to grant them a leave of absence for the trip. Still there were arguments, objections, reservations made and cancelled. But at last on April 1, 1930, the party sailed on the *President Roosevelt*—Polly Thomson, Anne Sullivan Macy, and Helen Keller.

12 * The British Isles and Europe

HELEN KELLER SMILED almost constantly as she walked the deck of the big ocean liner, adjusting her gait to its motion, or as she lay back in her deck chair between Polly and Anne. At night she slipped into her bunk and sleep came to her quickly, as she rocked gently back and forth, back and forth.

Their destination was being kept a secret so that they would have a real rest where they were going. Polly's sister had found them a cottage in Looe on the Cornish coast.

Helen thought she had never experienced such ease and freedom from responsibility. Life was suddenly idyllic, free from concerns.

Helen Keller did not quite realize that her whole life was in a way idyllic, surrounded by those who loved her. The friends that she enjoyed were nearly all extraordinary people who were filled with exceptional generosity and thought for others. She had never really worked in an

143

average group, where good and bad, honest and dishonest, selfish and generous are mingled together. She studied human misery and worked to end it, but she had never really lived in slum conditions or poverty herself. As a result, some of the things she has written do seem rather over-sweet, but they are a true representation of her thoughts. A trace of Little Lord Fauntleroy can be found in all of her thinking.

After the carefree days at sea, she and Polly and Anne were transferred to an automobile, and as their car spun along, Polly and Anne gave her word-pictures of the stretches of white beach, the bay, the many coves and inlets, the little fishing villages, the Cornish cottages of gray stone surrounded by flower gardens of purple fuchsias, white camellias, brilliant red geraniums.

Helen liked best to hear the word-pictures from Anne; it told her that Anne's vision was not yet completely gone.

The car began to climb and soon slowed to a halt before their ample cottage high on a cliff overlooking the Looe River. There the three women spent two peaceful months.

They spoke often of Ireland, even argued about it, because Helen and Polly wanted to go there and Anne did not. Anne was afraid to see the poverty that had driven her parents into exile, but at last she yielded, and at the end of June they went aboard a boat bound for Waterford.

Helen felt Anne's mood grow steadily darker, as they stood at the rail of the boat and then as they gradually traveled westward into Ireland. Green grass growing right to the water's edge, lush green hills, gray stone round towers that dated back more than a thousand years, castles fallen to ruin, old villages where the country folk brought their livestock to market once a week, farm women dressed in heavy brogans and long black dresses— Anne described it all for Helen, but to Anne it was too hopeless and backward to have any beauty. Helen sensed its beauty, but she had to admit that Ireland depressed her in a way that England had not.

The three were soon glad to leave Ireland and return to England, and for the remainder of their vacation they rented a country house in Essex.

"We cannot remain away from home forever," said one.

"No," said another.

Helen's correspondence was beginning to be full of information about the plans of the AFB for the first world conference on the blind. Reluctant to leave England but eager to be home for so significant a conference, they at last boarded an ocean liner bound for New York.

The winter season was crowded with work and events. In February Temple University conferred an honorary degree of Doctor of Humane Letters upon Helen Keller. Later the same month *Good Housekeeping* magazine published its list of America's twelve greatest women; one of them was Miss Keller.

In April delegates assembled at International House on Riverside Drive in New York City for the first World Conference on Work for the Blind.

As Helen Keller walked into the meeting hall, Mrs. Macy

at her side, she felt a flurry. The room was filled with human warmth. She clasped hand after hand: the blind Senator Thomas P. Gore of Oklahoma, Major M. C. Migel, President of the AFB, the Reverend Arthur William Blaxall of South Africa. There were representatives from thirty-seven nations, and they had come in response to an invitation issued by President Herbert Hoover.

Helen knew in her heart that she was the center of interest, the miracle they had come to see. That *was* her real function: drawing attention to the need and the hope.

Here at International House the scattered efforts of workers all over the world would begin to be coordinated, ideas and findings would be shared and taken back home, new courage and inspiration would be given to those who had begun to despair at the magnitude of the task.

Between sessions the Reverend Arthur William Blaxall drew her into conversation and told her about the progress and difficulties in his country.

"I hope you will pay South Africa a visit some day," he said.

She certainly wanted to go, and perhaps some day it would be possible. Just now, she explained, Mrs. Macy wasn't equal to it, and she couldn't leave her companion.

By summer the fifty-one-year-old Helen Keller and the sixty-five-year-old Anne Sullivan Macy were exhausted, and once more they decided on a European vacation. They spent it on the coast of France in the resort town of Concarneau, far out on the southern side of the Brittany Peninsula on the Bay of Biscay.

"Another idyllic vacation," said Miss Keller as she rested on the beach or hunted along the water's edge for interesting shells.

But it was not so for long. An urgent invitation came to her from the government of Yugoslavia, begging her to pay their country a visit and help them with a fund-raising campaign for the blind.

"It is out of the question," she said, but Anne Sullivan Macy insisted that she go.

"You are trying to spare me," was Mrs. Macy's accusation, and she was right.

This time Mrs. Macy won the argument, and the three women took a train for Belgrade in July. King Alexander himself entertained them at his summer palace. He accompanied Miss Keller on all her public appearances—a strenuous schedule of visits to meetings and schools—and for recreation took her on a boat ride on the Danube River. She had studied this river in her geography books as a child, and here she was floating on its waters, feeling the bow of the boat turn gently as the river curved.

Before she left Yugoslavia, the King decorated Helen Keller with the third order of St. Sava; upon Mrs. Macy he bestowed the fourth order, and upon Miss Thomson the fifth.

Fate decreed that Helen Keller was to have another trip to Europe for the third summer in a row. During the winter of 1931–1932 she received a cablegram from the University of Glasgow telling her that they wished to bestow upon her the honorary degree of Doctor of Laws. Recognition for the handicapped, for Anne Sullivan's faith, for women! It was rare for the University of Glasgow to bestow such a high honor upon a woman.

Soon a letter came from Dr. James Kerr Love, the Scottish surgeon with whom she had been corresponding for years. He offered her the hospitality of his home during her visit to Scotland.

Anne! Where was Anne? Anne was right at her side, and so was Polly. They were going to Scotland and then they were going to spend another long, lovely summer in the British Isles. Teacher could have a rest, and Polly Thomson could visit her family.

"You should smell the Scottish broom and the honey-suckle, the sweetbrier and the golden privet in June," Polly spelled into her hand.

"If we don't have to be in Glasgow until the middle of June, we can spend May in Looe," said Helen.

Once more the house was filled with happy planning and packing, and the three women sailed for England on April 27, 1932, going straight to a cottage in Looe. But Helen Keller's fame shattered the charm of Looe on this visit. She was beset and beseiged by reporters, invitations, mail, mail, mail, because everyone had read in the papers of the honorary degree.

Through all the excitement Helen sensed that Anne's strength was waning. Dear friend, she thought; dear, devoted friend . . .

The whirlwind at Looe was only a modest preview of

what was ahead of them in Scotland. Dr. and Mrs. James Kerr Love, who lived at West Kilbride on the Firth of Clyde, did their best. They arranged a separate cottage for the American visitors just a short train ride from Glasgow. But Helen's popularity was more than they could cope with, and because Helen Keller never thought of sparing herself, she plunged into a grueling schedule of visits and speeches at deaf and blind schools, diplomatic affairs, teas, and luncheons. It all needed to be done—to stimulate interest in the needs of the blind and the deaf.

Anne Sullivan Macy was at her side through a great deal of it, and that gave Helen a frequent twinge of worry.

She needed moral support from both Anne and Polly when the great presentation day arrived. Her old stage fright overtook her briefly on the fifteenth of June as she reached Bute Hall in Glasgow to receive her degree. She was breathing hard when Polly signaled her that it was her turn to walk forward to a set of steps, kneel upon a cushion, and feel the cap placed upon her head by the Dean of the Faculty of Law. He spoke in Latin, and she rose to her feet and gave her speech of acceptance, Teacher interpreting sentence by sentence.

"I accept the declaration of Glasgow University that darkness and silence need not bar the progress of the immortal spirit," were her closing words.

Later in the day she spoke again at the graduation exercises of Queen Margaret College, the women's college of the University of Glasgow.

There was one meeting that she particularly wanted to

fit into her schedule while she was in Scotland, and that was a meeting of the New Church of Scotland.

"The teachings of Emanuel Swedenborg have been my light and a staff in my hand, and by his vision splendid I am attended on my way."

Helen had learned to love Scotland, but another two weeks of official business awaited her in London.

"Perhaps you can return to Scotland after your London appointments," the Loves pleaded, and Helen held their hands tightly to assure them that she would try.

In London Helen, Anne, and Polly did have three blessed days of seclusion at the Park Lane Hotel. Only the Director of the National Institute for the Blind and Polly's sister, Margaret, knew they were in town.

Then the whirl began again—four and five appearances a day—and the energetic Miss Keller felt a great zest for it. She felt the power of one limousine after another, speeding her along, the bustle and stir when she joined another group. She clasped the hands of people about whom she had read a great deal, and read their personalities for herself. There were Sir Arthur and Lady Pearson, who had been sending her embossed books for many years.

"Now I can thank you personally," she said.

She clasped the hand of Lady Astor and found her "as charged with energy as an electric battery."

Soon she was talking with Bernard Shaw. He was "as bristling with egotism as a porcupine with quills. His handshake was quizzical and prickly, not unlike a thistle."

Her duties in London completed, there was another experience that Helen Keller wanted, and it had grown out of her voluminous reading. She wanted to visit the historic city of Canterbury and its cathedral. She had her wish, and her reactions to the big old cathedral were strictly her own. She liked best the tame doves that flew down and alighted about her and accepted crumbs of bread from her fingers.

While they were still in Canterbury, an extraordinary event caught them completely unawares. They returned to their hotel one afternoon to be told, "There is a call from your American Embassy in London. The Queen requests your presence at the Royal Garden Party at Buckingham Palace on July 21."

"But," protested Helen Keller innocently, "I have another engagement that afternoon, a large public meeting."

"Please, Miss Keller, an invitation from the Queen is a command. When it happens you are expected to cancel everything else."

"But that's tomorrow! How can I explain . . ."

"Please, Miss Keller, it needs no explanation in England."

She and her companions literally scrambled back to London on a morning train and out to Polly's sister's house in Hampstead to bathe and dress.

"Give me your chiffon dresses and I'll press them while you are bathing," said Margaret.

"My hat! My garden party hat!" gasped Helen. "I left it behind."

"We'll purchase one on the way to the party," declared Polly in her Scottish burr.

As soon as they were dressed, they rushed into a cab

and ordered the driver to go as quickly as possible to the shopping district. He stared at their flowing party gowns, but he did as he was told.

"Wait for us," one of them said in front of a store.

They disappeared inside and in five minutes they were back in the cab, a lovely big summer hat on Helen's head.

"Buckingham Palace, driver!"

"There is probably a special way, special rules of etiquette, and we haven't had time for any instruction," said Anne.

Procedures were explained to them when they arrived.

"Their Majesties will be told that you are here, and they will speak to you in time."

"Where are the King and Queen now?" demanded Helen. "How do they look?"

"They are standing under a red and gold canopy receiving guests," Polly told her. "The Queen is dressed in beige silk and carrying a sunshade of the same material."

"Is it a large party?"

"Oh, there are thousands here. It is a beautiful assembly. The flower gardens are in full bloom."

Just then an attendant approached them and said, "Will you ladies please come to the royal tent now?"

Helen talked to their Majesties through her companions and did not attempt to touch their lips.

"King George and Queen Mary are gracious and easy to talk to," Polly spelled into Helen's hand, "and intensely interested in you."

"The King wishes to see how we communicate with each other," said Anne.

Helen and her teacher chatted with one another to demonstrate both finger alphabet and lip reading.

"Are you enjoying your visit in England?" the Queen asked Helen Keller.

"It is a green and pleasant land," Helen Keller replied. "I love the beautiful English gardens."

"How can you enjoy the flowers if you do not see them?" asked the Queen.

"I smell their fragrance and feel their lovely forms."

In another few minutes the garden party that had so startled them was over, and Helen, Anne, and Polly returned to their round of appointments. As soon as their schedule was completed they fled from London to a rural cottage in Kent in southern England, there to catch their breath and talk over the rest of the summer.

"None of us has ever seen Paris," said Polly.

"Oh!" said Anne, brightening up for a second, but the next moment she wearily rested her head against the back of the chair. "I cannot." She was completely spent.

"Teacher cannot," said Helen, "and so we shall not."

"What of the Scottish Highlands?" Polly offered.

They had all thought often of Scotland since their visit with the Loves, and the decision to return was quickly made. They flew to Edinburgh, where another member of Polly's family met them and took them to the Caledonian Hotel on Princes Street. No responsibilities! No appointments! They could be tourists in this city of Robert Louis Stevenson, Sir Walter Scott, and Mary Queen of Scots, its ancient castle standing on a high granite rock right in the heart of town. When they had seen all they wished of Edinburgh, they boarded a train to tour the north of Scotland. A friend of the Thomsons gave them the use of his farmhouse in the Highlands, at South Arcan in the town of Muir-of-Ord in Ross County.

In South Arcan, in the peace of the moors and hills and pasturelands, the quiet nights, the soft, misty air, Helen Keller experienced a personal freedom that she had never found anywhere else.

> I walk every day alone, following old walls covered with lichens, mosses, and ferns. The figures of the bracken catch my dress as I pass, as if they would hold me fast. . . . I must disengage myself and move on to chat with the foxgloves and harebells. . . .

She spent nearly two months at South Arcan, and three important events highlighted her stay. She and her companions went on an exploring trip to the Island of Skye; they journeyed to Tarland, Aberdeenshire, to see Lord and Lady Aberdeen; and they went to Skibo Castle on Dornoch Firth to have luncheon with Mrs. Andrew Carnegie.

Dreams never last forever, and during the last week of September Helen, Anne, and Polly had to leave South Arcan and take a ship at Southampton bound for New York. A winter of work for the AFB awaited them.

Mrs. Macy could no longer work. Her sight was practically gone, and her physical strength was fading rapidly. The ailment that was slowly dragging her down had been diagnosed as an internal disorder, something she had to accept even though she felt a deep frustration at being so inactive.

Helen certainly could understand frustration, and she understood Anne's, particularly when Takeo Iwahashi paid her a visit.

Dr. Iwahashi was blind and was the most important worker for the blind in Japan; he eventually established a Lighthouse in Osaka.

How delicate and fine his hand was for a man's, Helen thought as she welcomed him, and yet how firm.

He had made his pilgrimage to Forest Hills to pay homage to Helen Keller and to ask her to come to Japan and stimulate interest there in the affairs of the blind.

She felt a quick twinge of excitement, but just as quickly she had to reconsider. "Mrs. Macy isn't able to travel," she told him, "and I cannot consider going without her."

Anne tried to insist, but Helen would not hear of it. Helen could travel with Polly! No, Helen replied firmly; she was not leaving Anne at this time.

By 1935 Helen could not take her any farther than the Catskills for a vacation, and the following summer the beaches of Long Island had to suffice.

That fall Anne spent her time partly in bed, partly sitting in a chair wrapped in blankets. One day when Polly brought her a cup of tea, Mrs. Macy asked, "Will you two come with me to Scotland next spring? I should be at peace there."

"I promise you that we shall go," said Helen, realizing full well that there might not be another spring for Anne.

Anne Sullivan Macy died in October. Even though Helen Keller was fully prepared for it, she felt utterly crushed. She had lost a part of herself. She could not seem to find her way around the house with her old self-confidence. She asked to be excused from all her public appearances. She idled her fingers over the keys of her braille writer or her typewriter and had no thoughts to marshal.

Teacher, dear devoted friend . . .

Polly Thomson was with her. Whenever Helen reached or groped before her, she felt the reassuring touch of Polly's hand. Polly read her the mail, attended to her personal needs, seemed always to be there.

But Anne Sullivan was gone and there would never be another like her.

Scarcely a week had passed after Anne's death when Polly began to talk to her about packing.

Packing? Why?

For a trip. Polly had been corresponding with her family, and arrangements were all made for a long visit with her brother in Glasgow, Scotland.

Scotland? Yes, of course! In Scotland, amidst the broom and heather, Helen Keller knew that she would find comfort and peace.

13 * The Blind of Other Lands

POLLY'S BROTHER, Robert J. Thomson, was a minister, and he and his wife took Helen to their manse and protected her from all visitors.

The misty air, the peaceful seclusion, quiet walks along footpaths bordered by fragrant shrubs, a visit to the Loves in West Kilbride, all helped to restore Helen Keller's well-being.

Life without Anne was different in many subtle ways, Helen realized. She had striven all her life to behave as nearly like a normal person as possible, and without Anne she would not have been able to come as far as she had. Anne's own blindness had helped her to understand Helen's. They had thought together through their fingers, and often a touch conveyed a whole idea. Of course, she was going on without Anne Sullivan Macy, but thoughts must be more carefully and fully expressed between herself and her present companions.

157

Soon after her arrival in Scotland she had returned to her regular morning task of reading and answering her mail. Many letters continued to come that contained thoughts of comfort and sympathy.

One morning in December a cablegram arrived that lighted something of her old spark. It was from Dr. Takeo Iwahashi, once more urging her to come to Japan and speak in behalf of the blind. The cable was soon followed by a long letter in braille. Would she please come in April? He recommended an itinerary that would take her through Japan, Korea, and Manchukuo. All hospitality was to be provided by the Japanese government. Whenever she traveled abroad on business trips, Helen Keller's expenses were paid for in a variety of ways: by the foreign governments, by interested organizations.

Slowly the idea began to take hold of Helen Keller's imagination. She recalled vividly Dr. Iwahashi's visit to Forest Hills and his first invitation to come to Japan. She had refused because of Teacher's ill health. One thought led to another. Before Dr. Iwahashi's visit there had been the Reverend Mr. Blaxall's invitation to journey to South Africa. So many blind in so many lands! They all needed her. Working for the blind of other lands would be an excellent balm for her grief, something that Anne would have wanted her to do, something she had almost forgotten that she herself wanted to do.

"Tell Mr. Iwahashi that I accept."

Helen and Polly returned to London at the end of January, crossed the Channel for a few days in Paris, and at Le Havre took the S.S. *Champlain* bound for New York.

During the trip home, and on the threshold of a whole new phase of her life, Helen Keller took the time to reflect and look back. Almost half a century had passed since the day that young Anne Sullivan had arrived in the little town of Tuscumbia. How far she had come since the day Teacher first handed her the blessed light of understanding and communication! How far all the blind, the deaf, and the deaf-blind had come in that half century! In 1887 there had been little public interest and almost no facilities or equipment for them. Now, in 1937, there were funds, organizations, schools, jobs, recreation centers, magazines, braille libraries, braille watches, braille games, Seeing-Eye dogs. The most recent invention was the "talking book" for the blind, a phonograph record of a trained voice reading the full text of a book. She had mentioned the "talking book" in her public speeches in Paris a few days back, and the French people had shown intense interest. And there was radio. What a boon to the sightless!

The American Foundation for the Blind had been in operation for fourteen years, and it was responsible for a great deal of the progress that had been made. It had done a tremendous job of educating the public. It had encouraged legislation all over the country. It was directly responsible for the section of the Social Security Act providing relief for the needy blind, and for national laws providing funds for free braille books and talking-book machines and records.

On Long Island the Industrial Home for the Blind had

been working for more than forty years with the adult blind. The IHB had been founded by Eben Porter Morford in 1893. Mr. Morford had lost his sight at seventeen as the result of a street accident; and, after he had completed his re-education at the New York Institute for the Blind, he discovered how few job opportunities there were for him. If there were no job opportunities for him, then what about other blind adults? He and a group of his friends made this particular need their responsibility and began a small factory for the caning of chairs by blind workers. It grew rapidly and soon added such other products as brooms and mattresses. Next, it developed training courses for teaching trades to adult blind persons and training courses to teach them to go about streets unattended, to look after themselves, to keep house—in other words to be independent and self-respecting.

What a complex task it was. There were thousands of handicapped in the United States alone, not to mention those in every other country of the world, and yet no two were ever alike. Every one was an individual. There were the totally blind who saw only blackness; there were those who could distinguish between light and dark, those who could make out large objects, those with a small degree of vision who could read large block letters. A person was legally blind if he saw less at a distance of twenty feet than a person with normal vision could see at two hundred feet.

There were just as many degrees of deafness, and there was every combination of the two handicaps: a few totally deaf and totally blind like herself, some totally deaf and partially blind, others hard of hearing and blind.

Tremendous strides had been made in teaching methods. Youngsters in the deaf-blind division of Perkins Institution now were taught with far greater skill and greater success than when she had attended the school. They were taught speech from the start, and they learned to understand it through the Vibration Method. They felt sounds by laying their fingers on the teacher's face and throat. They felt sounds on the piano, and learned the difference between high and low tones. Gradually they learned words through simple commands: bow, run, walk, come, go; and they learned the basic sounds from which words are made: oh, ah, oo, ee, aye, and the consonants. Sound is vibration, and in a normal person it reaches the understanding through the ears. It reaches the understanding of a deaf person through his finger tips.

At Perkins the children developed their sense of touch by handling every kind of object: smooth boards, sandpaper, silk, cotton, wool, squares, balls; and they learned to fold, tie knots, string beads, weave, knit, model clay. As soon as a child was ready, he began to use block letters and braille, and he progressed through the same subjects as a normal child: reading, spelling, geography, arithmetic, history. The only difference was that all his textbooks were in braille. Graduating from Perkins was the equivalent of graduating from high school.

As a result of the new teaching methods, a deaf-blind person could converse with a normal person by holding his fingers on the lips and face of the other person to "hear" what he said. The finger alphabet was still taught as an extra tool, and another very simple method was to trace block letters in the palm.

Other schools for the blind or the deaf in the United States were beginning to develop deaf-blind divisions. (Today there are seven in addition to Perkins, in the states of Alabama, Illinois, Iowa, New York, California, Michigan, and Washington.) Their particular need was for specially trained teachers. Since every doubly handicapped child's case was different, he could not be taught in a class or group. One teacher was needed for every two children.

Realizing that she must not hope to solve all the problems of the blind and deaf herself, and remembering that there were many capable and dedicated people working in the field, Helen Keller turned her thoughts once more to the next task before her: the blind of other lands. As soon as she reached Forest Hills she must begin preparing for her trip to the Orient.

She did not arrive home until the tenth of February, and by the end of March she was on her way to San Francisco, where she went aboard the *Asama Maru* on the first of April, carrying a letter of greeting to the Japanese people from President Franklin D. Roosevelt. Since he himself knew the anguish of a physical handicap, he was deeply interested in Helen Keller's work.

From the day she left California until she returned, the East spoke to her in the language of flowers, and anywhere in the world where flowers were the language of love and hospitality Helen Keller was at home. There were huge bouquets of flowers from the Japanese of California to see her off, and when the *Asama Maru* stopped at Honolulu, Hawaii, beautiful *leis*, or large wreaths, were placed about her neck. Happily her fingers explored every gift of flowers and held them to her face. Before she left Hawaii the Territorial School for the Deaf and the Blind sent her a bouquet containing the typical flowers of the islands, and to each blossom was attached a card in braille giving its name and colorings. She knew she would reach Japan in time for the cherry blossom festival.

The *Asama Maru* arrived in Tokyo Bay in the middle of April, and Polly Thomson stood at Helen's side describing everything in detail.

"A motor launch full of officialdom is approaching the ship, and I see Dr. Iwahashi among them. They are all smiling. I never saw such smiling people."

"Hail, beautiful Japan!" Helen said in her first speech. "I wish to begin some small work in the service of the blind people of this beautiful country. . . ."

The cherry blossoms almost defeated Polly's supply of words. "Clouds," she told Helen. "Pink clouds of blossoms everywhere, and amongst the branches I see a shrine with its tier upon tier of delicately curving roofs."

In Tokyo Helen and Polly were swept along on a tidal wave of hospitality that ended in a garden party at the Imperial Palace where they were presented to the Emperor and Empress. From Tokyo they went on southward, taking the eight-hour train trip to Osaka, another big city.

Japan was a small country that teemed with people. Helen was thrilled to experience a whole new racial temperament. She felt their small, exquisite hands, their gentle dispositions, and she became quickly aware of their great love for children.

By the end of July she and her party reached Dairen on the tip of the Liaotung Peninsula in the Yellow Sea, and from there they went to Hsinking in central Manchukuo. Manchukuo was under Japanese rule; in fact, the Second Sino-Japanese War was still going on. Because of the war Helen Keller decided not to visit China and sailed from Yokohama for home on the twelfth of August.

"Home to Forest Hills and a lovely rest," she and Polly agreed, on the way back across the United States.

But Forest Hills, for so long a secluded and quiet place, ignored and hard to reach, had begun to stir. The outside world was invading the marshes and meadows with railway tracks and subway lines and elaborate plans for a World's Fair.

Helen Keller knew she must find another retreat, and her friends agreed. Mr. Gustavus Pfeiffer, of the Richard Hudnut cosmetics company, invited her to live in Easton, Connecticut, near Westport. The home of his nephew, Professor Robert Pfeiffer, was vacant for the time being, and she was welcome to use it, he told her. Eagerly she accepted his protection.

Mr. Pfeiffer, "Uncle Gus" to Helen, gave her seven acres of land in Easton and built her a home there. It was a colonial style house, nine rooms, painted white with green shutters. So that she could "see" the whole house, he had a scale model made of it that was about three feet long and a foot high, and presented it to her at a party of fifty of her closest associates.

Happily she explored her new home with her finger tips, and when asked what she would name it she replied, "I have thought about that a great deal. I shall call it 'Arcan Ridge' after the farmhouse in South Arcan, Scotland, where Teacher and I were so happy together."

As soon as she and Polly and servants were settled in "Arcan Ridge," Helen Keller resumed a task that she had been working on whenever she could for the past several years: her life of Anne Sullivan Macy. She had a wealth of letters, diaries, and notes, and she turned to them whenever her tasks for the AFB gave her free time.

The AFB wanted her to go to more foreign countries, and so did she, but the same autumn that she took possession of "Arcan Ridge" the armies of Hitler took possession of Poland. There could be no more travel until World War II was ended. She soon found herself visiting deafened and blinded war veterans once more. In 1944 the AFB sent her on a nationwide tour of army hospitals to cheer the patients and advise those who were caring for them.

She was sixty-five on the twenty-seventh of June, 1945, and the Industrial Home for the Blind gave a tea in her honor at its Brooklyn headquarters. Dr. Peter J. Salmon, the Executive Director, was her host. Helen Keller's face was wreathed with smiles during the tea, because the IHB took the occasion to announce the opening of its new deaf-blind department.

On one of her visits to New York a remarkable young man paid her a call. He was Robert J. Smithdas, totally deaf and blind like herself, and a Perkins graduate. He had come to tell her that he was realizing his dream of going to college. He was going to sit in classes at St. John's University in Brooklyn with a companion spelling the lectures into his hand, just as she had once done at Radcliffe. When he completed his schooling he wanted to be a writer.

"You will succeed at both," she assured him.

Mr. Smithdas did complete his four years at St. John's and then took a master's degree at New York University. That accomplished, he became a staff counselor at the headquarters of the Industrial Home for the Blind. His speech is clear and understandable, and he is much less dependent on a companion than Miss Keller, because he has had the advantage of the progress that has been made in teaching techniques, and because he did not lose his hearing at quite so early an age as she. His autobiography, *Life at My Fingertips*, tells his whole interesting story.

As soon as World War II had ended, Helen Keller resumed her work for the blind of the world, and the newly formed American Foundation for Overseas Blind played a big part in planning her trips. The AFOB had formerly been called the American Braille Press, and it became a sister organization of the AFB with practically the same Board and the same executive directors.

In the autumn of 1946 she set out by plane on a trip to London, Paris, and Rome, visiting hospitals and schools for the blind all along the way.

While she was in Rome she received the startling news that "Arcan Ridge" had burned to the ground. For a long moment she couldn't believe it. Everything was gone—the house and all its furnishings, some of them treasures given to her in Japan, all her letters and papers and braille library, her manuscript of Teacher's biography.

"It was three-fourths written," she said to Polly.

There had been no one in the house at the time. A neighbor had noticed flames around the chimney and called the fire department, but the fire had already taken hold.

Helen and Polly had to rally themselves and complete their tour. Returning through Germany, by November, 1947, they had arrived in England, where Queen Elizabeth, wife of George VI, granted them an audience. A few days before Christmas they reached Connecticut, where the charred ruins of their home awaited them.

Their worldly goods had been destroyed, but not the devotion of their friends. Helen learned almost at once that a small group was working quietly to rebuild "Arcan Ridge" for her. Only ten months later she took possession of her restored home. The new "Arcan Ridge" was built along the same lines as the old and on the exact same site, far back from the road on a rise of land, sheltered from public view by huge trees and luxurious shrubs.

Spring found her on the world travel lanes once more:

Hawaii, Australia, Japan, and in 1950 she was in Paris for her seventieth birthday.

The following year an old, old dream came true. She made the long journey to South Africa that the Reverend Mr. Arthur Blaxall had suggested nearly twenty years before. Under the auspices of the South African National Council for the Blind, the South African National Council for the Deaf, and the AFOB, Miss Keller, Miss Thomson, and Mr. Alfred Allen of the AFOB, arrived by ship at Cape Town the middle of March. Mr. Blaxall, who was in charge of Helen's trip, was there with the mayor and his officials— and the cheering throngs—to welcome them.

"It may well be that this tour will prove to be the climax of my life," Helen Keller told the assembled multitude.

The crowds followed her and milled around her car all the way to Mount Nelson Hotel for her press interviews. As she patiently answered question after question, no matter how many times before it had been asked her during her life, she knew she was plunging into another new experience in racial temperaments. What a profound influence environment had on human personalities! How attitudes differed in different places!

She had done a great deal of reading on South Africa before her trip, and she was prepared for the segregation that she found and for the fact that it often doubled the work she must do. After her tea at the Dominican School for White Deaf, for instance, she attended a second tea at the Dominican School for Colored Deaf. She was grieved about the separateness. Running two deaf schools was twice as costly as one, and the separateness could only increase human suffering.

Her South African itinerary took her over nearly seven thousand miles. In nine weeks she visited twenty-eight schools and spoke at forty-eight meetings and receptions. Everywhere that she went the response in enthusiasm and cash donations to the two national councils for work with the blind was tremendous.

"You have aroused the consciences of many," the Reverend Blaxall told her gratefully.

A touching scene occurred toward the end of her tour, when she was aboard a train returning to Cape Town. As the train neared Worcester, where earlier in her visit she had spent some time at a large school for deaf children, she received word that the children had all come down to the railway fence to see her once more.

"Open the window," she insisted, and as the train slowed down and crept past the school grounds, Helen Keller leaned far out the window and waved. The children thronged against the fencing and waved and cheered to her, even though they knew she could neither see nor hear.

Her African journey was by no means her last foreign adventure. During the next five years she toured the Near East, Latin America, India. Everywhere she was received enthusiastically; everywhere she found new homes, schools, and workshops for the blind being established. She was almost seventy-seven when she set out on a tour of Finland and Norway.

14 * Memory Pictures in My Fingers

"ARCAN RIDGE," with its privacy, was her retreat between journeys. There she lived modestly and simply while gifts, honors, and awards fell about her like snow-flakes, and there she wrote one more important book: a whole new life of Anne Sullivan Macy, a searching story of their long personal experience together, a tribute to "Teacher" from "the foster-child of her mind." Doubleday published it in 1956.

Teacher, Anne Sullivan Macy was written entirely from memory, without the papers that had been destroyed in the fire, a memory living entirely on images that had reached it through Helen's sensitive finger tips.

Her seeing, hearing finger tips held a wealth of memory pictures—people, creatures, things, places—hands of the great and the humble that she had grasped, dogs of every shape and description, faces of children crowded around her in all the costumes of the globe, flowers, houses and furnishings, books, fallen columns of ruined temples, priceless art objects.

170

She fluttered her fingers constantly as she walked along, because that was how she reflected, investigated, and remembered. She would flutter her fingers to recall an idea or name momentarily forgotten, or she would step out of doors and flutter her fingers in the air to judge the weather.

Helen Keller lived in almost complete retirement now. Her friend and companion, Polly Thomson, died on March 20, 1960, and Mrs. Winifred Corbally came to take her place. Even in retirement Miss Keller lived a full life. Each morning she went over the mail and answered a great deal of it on her typewriter. Later the newspapers and periodicals were read to her. In the afternoon she took a walk on the grounds of "Arcan Ridge," feeling her way along the fences and guide lines that had been built to permit her to go out alone. She grew frail as she approached her eighty-eighth birthday, and she did not quite reach it. During the afternoon of June 1, 1968, as she lay dozing, she slipped quietly away into death.

Because she had lived such a dedicated and useful life, Helen Keller enjoyed a deep inner peace. Her personality radiated happiness and contentment. Her whole life had been a guide and inspiration to thousands of others.

Once a reporter asked her this question through her companion, "Does Dr. Helen Keller feel that she has really achieved anything in her life?"

Helen Keller replied immediately, "I believe that all through these dark and silent years God has been using my life for a purpose I do not know, but one day I shall understand, and then I will be satisfied."

How to Behave with a Deaf, a Blind, or a Deaf-Blind Person

WHATEVER A PERSON's handicaps, be kind, gentle, considerate, serious, and absolutely trustworthy. Remember that he is a human being just like you with the same kinds of feelings. He is just as mature, dignified, and intelligent as you, and maybe much more so. The first step is to discover how to talk with him.

If he is deaf, move in front of him so that he can see you. Perhaps he can read your lips when you talk, or perhaps he knows the finger alphabet. If you can't use the finger alphabet with him, you can write him notes with pencil and paper, or you can draw block letters into the palm of his hand.

If he is blind, speak to him so that he can tell where you are. Don't shout; he isn't deaf. If you are walking with him, let *him* take *your* arm. The motion of your body

172

usually lets him know what to expect. If you are eating together, ask him *if* he wants help, such as cutting his meat. When you guide him to a chair merely put his hand on the arm or back of it and let him seat himself. In *his* house leave all the furniture and other things exactly where he knows they are. In a strange house tell him where things are and who is present. Never pet or distract a Seeing Eye dog.

If he is deaf and blind, you must touch him to let him know you are there. A pat on his arm between shoulder and elbow means here-I-am, or hello, or you-are-right, or any number of reassuring remarks. If he is young he has probably gone to a special school and knows the Vibration Method. In that case let him place his fingers on your lips and cheek and speak to him slowly, clearly, and loudly enough to make plenty of vibrations. He probably knows the finger alphabet, or here again you can draw block letters in his palm.

On the next page is a series of pictures showing the finger alphabet. It is easy to learn, and you never can tell when you may need it.

THE
ONE-HAND ALPHABET
USED BY
DEAF-BLIND PEOPLE

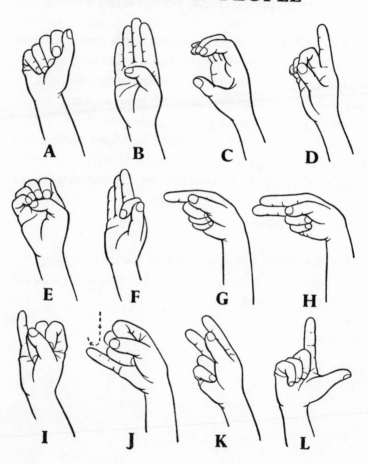

A   B   C   D

E   F   G   H

I   J   K   L

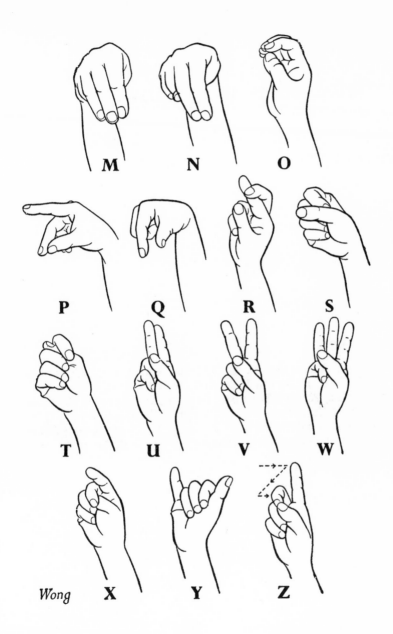

M   N   O

P   Q   R   S

T   U   V   W

Wong   X   Y   Z

Selected Bibliography

BOOKS

ALLEN, ALEXANDER V. G. *Phillips Brooks, 1835–1893.* New York: E. P. Dutton & Co., Inc., 1907.

BLAXALL, ARTHUR WILLIAM. *Helen Keller under the Southern Cross.* Cape Town and Johannesburg: Juta & Co., Ltd., 1952.

BRADDY, NELLA. *Anne Sullivan Macy, The Story Behind Helen Keller.* Garden City: Doubleday, Doran & Company, Inc., 1933.

BROOKS, VAN WYCK. *Helen Keller, Sketch for a Portrait.* New York: E. P. Dutton & Co., Inc., 1956.

DAVIDSON, DONALD. *The Tennessee.* New York: Rinehart & Co., Inc., 1946.

FRENCH, RICHARD SLAYTON. *From Homer to Helen Keller.* New York: The American Foundation for the Blind, Inc., 1932.

HENDERSON, LOIS T. *The Opening Doors, My Child's First Eight Years Without Sight.* New York: The John Day Company, 1954.

KELLER, HELEN. *Helen Keller's Journal, 1936–1937*. Garden City: Doubleday, Doran & Company, Inc., 1938.

———. *Helen Keller in Scotland, A Personal Record Written by Herself*. London: Methuen & Co., Ltd., 1933.

———. *Midstream, My Later Life*. Garden City: Doubleday, Doran & Company, Inc., 1929.

———. *My Religion*. New York: Swedenborg Foundation, Inc., 1956.

———. *Out of the Dark: Essays, Letters, and Addresses on Physical and Social Vision*. Garden City: Doubleday, Page & Company, 1913.

———. *The Song of the Stone Wall*. New York: The Century Co., 1910.

———. *The Story of My Life*. Garden City: Doubleday & Company, Inc., 1955.

———. *Teacher, Anne Sullivan Macy*. Garden City: Doubleday & Company, Inc., 1956.

———. *The World I Live In*. New York: The Century Co., 1908.

LAMSON, MARY SWIFT. *Life and Education of Laura Dewey Bridgman*. Boston: Houghton Mifflin Company, 1881.

MACKENZIE, CATHERINE. *Alexander Graham Bell, The Man Who Contracted Space*. New York: Grosset & Dunlap, Inc., 1928.

ROCHELEAU, CORINNE, AND MACK, REBECCA. *Those in the Dark Silence*. Washington: Volta Bureau, 1930.

ROSS, ISHBEL. *Journey into Light*. New York: Appleton-Century-Crofts, Inc., 1951.

SCHWARTZ, HAROLD. *Samuel Gridley Howe*. Cambridge: Harvard University Press, 1956.

SMITHDAS, ROBERT. *Life at My Fingertips*. Garden City: Doubleday & Company, Inc., 1958.

TROBRIDGE, GEORGE. *Swedenborg, Life and Teaching*. New York: Swedenborg Foundation, Inc., 1955.

ZAHL, PAUL A. (editor). *Blindness, Modern Approaches to the Unseen Environment*. Princeton: Princeton University Press, 1950.

MAGAZINE ARTICLES

American Anthropologist: HITZ, JOHN. "Helen Keller." April–June, 1906.

California Parent-Teacher: LOWENFELD, BERTHOLD. "If Deaf and Blind." April, 1952.

Journal of Abnormal and Social Psychology: GOODENOUGH, FLORENCE L. "Expression of the Emotions in a Blind-Deaf Child." October–December, 1932.

———: MERRY, RALPH V. "A Case Study in Deaf-Blindness." July–September, 1930.

Journal of Exceptional Children: HALL, INIS B. "Practical Treatment of the Deaf-Blind." April, 1937.

Ladies' Home Journal: KELLER, HELEN. "My Future as I See It." November, 1903.

———: MACY, JOHN ALBERT. "Helen Keller as She Really Is." October and November, 1902.

McClure's Magazine: KELLER, HELEN. "An Apology for Going to College." June, 1905.

The New Outlook for the Blind: DINSMORE, ANNETTE B. "National Approach to the Education of Deaf-Blind Children." January, 1954.

Outlook for the Blind: BRYAN, DOROTHY. "Work Opportunities for the Deaf-Blind." October, 1949.

———: KELLER, HELEN. "John Hitz as I Knew Him." July, 1908.

St. Nicholas Magazine: ELLIS, WILLIAM T. "Helen Keller and Tommy Stringer." October, 1897.

———: HALL, FLORENCE HOWE. "Helen Keller." September, 1889.

The Saturday Evening Post: MURRAY, DON. "What Do You Mean by 'Hopeless'?" March 2, 1957.

The Volta Review: ALCORN, SOPHIA. "The Tadoma Method." May, 1932.

———: DALEY, JANE B. "The Value of Vibration in Teaching Speech to the Deaf." May, 1932.

———: HALL, INIS B. "The Education of the Blind-Deaf." October, 1940.

The Youth's Companion: KELLER, HELEN. "My Story." January 4, 1894.

PAMPHLETS

DINSMORE, ANNETTE B. *Methods of Communication with Deaf-Blind People.* New York: American Foundation for the Blind, Educational Series No. 5, 1953.

FARRELL, GABRIEL. *Children of the Silent Night.* Watertown: Perkins School for the Blind, 1956.

FISH, ANNA GARDNER. *Perkins Institution and Its Deaf-Blind Pupils.* Watertown: Perkins Institution and Massachusetts School for the Blind, 1934.

FULLER, SARAH. *How Helen Keller Was Taught Speech.* Washington: Volta Bureau, 1905.

MYKLEBUST, HELMER R. *The Deaf-Blind Child.* Watertown: Perkins School for the Blind, 1956.

INDEX

180

About the Author

Catherine Owens Peare was born in New Jersey and was graduated from New Jersey State College at Montclair. As an adult she lived for many years in Brooklyn, New York, and is now a resident of Connecticut.

She has always been keenly interested in writing. She was editor of her high school paper and a contributor to the literary quarterly of her college. Miss Peare is the author of a long list of biographies for young people including Albert Einstein, Mary McLeod Bethune, William Penn, Louis Agassiz, The FDR Story, The Woodrow Wilson Story, and The Herbert Hoover Story. The Helen Keller Story remains the great favorite with children. It received Oklahoma's Sequoyah Award, and in Kansas it was selected for the William Allen White Award. Winners for both of these literary prizes are chosen by children.

Miss Peare has always considered travel an essential part of her writing task, and her research has taken her to many parts of the United States and to thirteen foreign countries.